The Focused Interview

THE
FOCUSED
INTERVIEW

A Manual of
Problems and Procedures

SECOND EDITION

BY

ROBERT K. MERTON
MARJORIE FISKE
PATRICIA L. KENDALL

THE FREE PRESS
A Division of Macmillan, Inc.
NEW YORK

Collier Macmillan Publishers
LONDON

The Free Press
A Division of Macmillan, Inc.
866 Third Avenue, New York, N. Y. 10022

Collier Macmillan Canada, Inc.

Printed in the United States of America

printing number

1 2 3 4 5 6 7 8 9 10

Library of Congress Cataloging-in-Publication Data

Merton, Robert King
  The focused interview: a manual of problems and procedures / by
Robert K. Merton, Marjorie Fiske, Patricia L. Kendall.—2nd ed.
      p.   cm.
  Includes bibliographical references.
  ISBN 0-02-920985-4. — ISBN 0-02-920986-2 (pbk.)
  1. Focused group interviewing. 2. Marketing research.
I. Lowenthal, Marjorie Fiske. II. Kendall, Patricia L. III. Title.
H61.28.M47   1990
658.8′3—dc20   90-30322
                                                         CIP

TO PAUL

Contents

Foreword

Classic works of scholarship may be viewed either as monuments or as stepping stones. In the former case a historical relic whose value is assessed mainly in the context of its time is held up for veneration. In the latter case, attention is directed to the vital contribution made by a work to *cumulative* knowledge and progress. Rarely can close scrutiny of a classic be recommended for both its historical value and its contemporary utility. *The Focused Interview* is one such case.

More than forty years have passed since this work began to be formulated at the Bureau of Applied Social Research (BASR), then in its first decade of existence at Columbia University. First and foremost, the report is a useful guide to individual and group interviewing, shaped by a sophisticated grasp both of theories of social exchange and of the scientific requirements for gathering data and testing hypotheses. It is also a testimonial to the uniquely fruitful collaboration of BASR founder Paul F. Lazarsfeld, with his life-long colleague, Robert K. Merton, as well as with Patricia Kendall. Thus, the book (and Merton's illuminating new introduction) will be of great interest to historians of the social sciences.

An historical perspective can also shed light on factors influencing research developments since the 1940s, particularly on research trends in many fields of application: advertising, marketing, and political or public opinion research.

Much of our knowledge of social, political, and economic life over this period was gained through interview surveys, a mode of active intervention shaped by specific needs and governed by pragmatically developed rules. "Conversations with a purpose" or "guided conversations," as the method was called, replaced ad hoc modes of questioning that ignored the Heisenbergian effects of the inquiry upon the information gathered.

Systematic research on the interview method blossomed in the 1940s, as both academic and commercial investigators turned to surveys as an important means of achieving quantified results—then as now recognized as a certifier of scientific knowledge. But the interest in quantification was not simply a matter of academic status-striving or commercial self-promotion. It was written by urgent social needs. As Merton reminds us, nothing propelled the search for accuracy in achieving quantified findings based on interviews more than the exigencies of fostering both civilian and military morale during World War II.

Analytically considered, interviewing as a method contains a paradox, combining a quest for detailed knowledge about individual beliefs, activities, and sentiments—often of a burdensome, intimate, or emotion-arousing nature—with a need to assess these subjective phenomena within a framework that permits rigorous comparison and quantitative analysis. The former requires establishing a friendly rapport between the two parties to this transient relationship, one that fosters credibility and a free flow of accurate information in response to careful questioning. (Achievement of rapport can, of course, be facilitated or limited by the sociocultural context). The interviewer actively collaborates in the process, and her judgment and social skills are essential to its success.

In contrast, the emphasis on quantification inclines this process in a narrower, more circumscribed direction, in which the exchanges of meaning that define social relationships are limited to the greatest possible degree. The interviewer here is like the scalpel or the microscope: a passive tool employed by the investigator with only marginal effects on the fact-finding process. In actual fact, as we know, sample surveys embody elements of both. Thus the key to securing the advantages of the former while achieving the rigor of the latter lies in the *codification of procedures*. This codification was and remains the chief achievement of *The Focused Interview*.

Scientific progress over the past forty years has transformed the attitude survey into a marvelously flexible instrument. Sampling of both mass populations and rare segments has been routinized by computers and the use of the telephone as a screening device. Data gathering has been compressed from weeks or days to hours, thanks to computer-assisted telephone interviewing. Analysis of survey data has also been transformed by computerized statistical programs. Instantaneous readouts of poll results are now possible, based on mass "interviews" with as many as 1,200 people at one time, responding by means of hand-held computerized devices. (This development was based in stepping-stone fashion on a primitive recording device pioneered at BASR, the Lazarsfeld-Stanton Program Analyzer. As Merton notes, that device figured prominently in the research assignment that ultimately led to the production of this book.)

Progress on all of these fronts has secured a place for quantification as a leading mode of knowledge production in the social sciences and allied fields. But at the same time, many clients of applied survey research (agencies as well as individuals) have become resistant to quantitative studies. The strength of the method, namely, its capacity to provide timely, precise measures of a wide variety of social facts, does not suit them when they search for clues to motives for behavior or potential points of leverage. The human element that helps one to translate social facts into policy recommendations often appears to be missing in massive quantitative portraits and analyses, and one result has been that qualitative research—most notably in the form of "focus groups"—has assured greater prominence in many fields of application including politics, commerce (advertising and marketing), and communications.

But just as quantitative survey research based on the interview was significantly advanced by this book, so too were qualitative approaches. In fact (as Merton's introduction indicates), focus groups themselves are grounded in the technique of the focused interview, as described in Chapter VII, "The Group Interview." Moreover, as the reading of a 1985 Advertising Research Foundation publication, "Focus Groups: Issues and Approaches," will attest, that chapter's formulation of the advantages and dsiadvantages of group interviews has not been much improved upon. But focus group interviewing (unlike individual interviewing) has not generated any significant body of research concerning its reliability and validity. Thus the "craft" element in its use remains much greater than with individual interviewing. For this reason, this book's sophisticated approach to the problems of securing relevant responses in group interviews continues to offer a sturdy guidepost for the contemporary researcher.

As the scope of the interview survey has grown, the research process has become increasingly bureaucratized: consequently, the responses sought become more stereotyped and further removed from natural modes of discourse. We therefore run the risk of losing sight of the seemingly simple social interaction process of asking and answering questions. Fortunately, a close study of *The Focused Interview* reveals how it is possible, even in interview surveys of great range and complexity, to seek out and to capture the authentic human voice.

Albert E. Gollin
Newspaper Advertising Bureau
New York City

Introduction to the Second Edition

The reappearance of this book after so many years offers a welcome opportunity to address a new generation of readers—students and research practitioners who are far removed from the era in which it took shape. This introduction enables me to make some comments on that most sociological of questions, "How did it come to be so?" by ransacking the past in the search for answers. That quest, in turn, was taken up several years ago by a serendipitous invitation to speak on a topic requiring some impromptu historical research, in order to trace apparent links between the subject of this book and the subsequent emergence of "focus groups."

There can't be many people in the field of social science and certainly none in the related field of marketing research who know less about focus groups than I. So it was that when Alan Meyer, president of the New York chapter of AAPOR, broached the subject of focus groups to me, he enlisted my curiosity. It had been only a little while ago that Patricia Kendall and I had learned of the widespread use of focus groups in marketing research. Perhaps we had not been reading the "right" books and journals. At any rate, when this develop-

Public Opinion Quarterly Volume 51:550–566 © 1987 by the American Association for Public Opinion Research. Published by The University of Chicago Press / 0033-362X/87/0051-04 (1). Originally published in a slightly different form.

ment was called to our attention and when the techniques employed in focus-group research were said to derive from our work some forty years ago on the focussed interview of groups (Merton and Kendall, 1946; Merton, Fiske, and Kendall, 1956), my own curiosity about that development began to mount. Still, I did little to gratify that curiosity at the time. Other research questions and problems were occupying my attention. And as the literary philosopher Kenneth Burke once observed (in a memorable fashion that I like to describe as the Burke theorem) : "A way of seeing is also a way of not seeing—a focus upon object A involves a neglect of object B." (That maxim, by the way, is clearly one to be remembered in the use of focussed interviews and focus groups).

And so when Alan Meyer invited me to speak to the New York chapter of AAPOR about that subject, I couldn't resist the multiple temptations he had put before me. But now I want to translate his invitation into cognitive terms, which he may not recognize. This is my interpretation of his subtext and my reconstruction of what was contained in that invitation: "Here is a grand opportunity to meet with a group of accomplished and informed social researchers, many of them your old friends, drawn partly from the universities and partly from that world of marketing research to which Paul Lazarsfeld introduced you half a century ago. Here is an opportunity also to combine a newly emerging interest in the origins and rapid growth of focus-group research with your lifelong interest in identifying various patterns in the emergence and transmission of knowledge, particularly in the diffusion of knowledge from one sociocultural world to another. How are ideas conveyed and how are they modified in the course of diffusion? What can be learned about patterns of change in the diffusion of innovations from science into practice? Having devoted a great part of your life to studies in the sociology of science—though, unlike Paul Lazarsfeld, rather less to the sociology of social science—you now have an opportunity to reflect aloud, to speculate, about this sort of thing in connection with the emergence and growth of focus-group research."

The impromptitude of my remarks on that occasion held for the specific subject. The underlying questions I wanted to address were enduring and not very well understood ones; surely not well understood by me and, I suspect, not by many others.

It all started in my first inadvertent work session—a thoroughly unplanned work session—with Paul Lazarsfeld back in November 1941. That story has been told in print several times (Hunt, 1961; Lazarsfeld, 1975:35–37; De Lellio, 1985: 21–24), but never in tracing the seedbed of the focussed interview. I retell it here in that new context.

To begin with, Paul and I had never heard of one another before coming to Columbia. We had not only not read one another; we had literally never heard of one another. But in November 1941, Paul, as the elder of us, invited the Mertons to dinner. He met us at the door and said something like this: "Bob, I have wonderful news for you. I've just gotten a call from the O.F.F. in Washington [that was the Office of Facts and Figures, which was the predecessor of the Office of War Information, which in turn was, I believe, the predecessor of the Voice of America]. They want me to do some tests of responses to several radio morale programs. So here's a great opportunity for you. Come with me to the studio to see how we test audience response."

Thus it was that Paul dragged me into the strange world of radio research—back in those early days, unknown to just about everyone and surely so to me. I knew that Paul headed up something called the Office of Radio Research but I knew nothing about its work. So off we went and then it was that I came upon a strange spectacle. Do try to see it through my then naïve eyes and remember that our present sophistication is the legacy of almost half a century of evolving inquiry. I enter a radio studio for the first time, and there I see a smallish group—a dozen, or were there twenty?—seated in two or three rows. Paul and I take our places as observers at the side of the room as unobstrusively as we can; there is no one-way mirror or anything of that sort. These people are being asked to press a red button on their chairs when anything they hear on the recorded radio program evokes a negative response—irritation, anger, disbelief, boredom—and to press a green button when they have a positive response. For the rest, no buttons at all. I soon learn that their cumulative responses are being registered on a primitive polygraph consisting of the requisite number of fountain pens connected by sealing wax and string, as it were, to produce cumulative curves of signaled likes and dislikes. That primitive instrument became known as the Lazarsfeld-Stanton program analyzer. We then observe one of Paul's assistants questioning the test-group—the audience—about their "reasons" for their recorded likes and dislikes. I begin passing notes to Paul about what I take to be great deficiencies in the interviwer's tactics and procedures. He was not focussing sufficiently on *specifically* indicated reactions, both individual and aggregated. He was inadvertently guiding responses; he was not eliciting spontaneous expressions of earlier responses when segments of the radio program were being played back to the group. And so on and on. For although this is a new kind of interview situation for me, I am not unfamiliar with the art and craft of interviewing. For one thing, I had spent more time than I care to remember during the summer of 1932 when I was a graduate student at Harvard, helping to keep myself alive by working on a WPA project devoted to interviewing just about all the hoboes and homeless men and women that could be located in the Boston area. Having had the experience of interviewing under those sometimes strenuous conditions, this situation strikes me as providing almost privileged access to people's states of mind and affect.

At any rate, after the interview is over, Paul asks me: "Well what did you think of it?" I proceed to express my interest in the general format and to reiterate, at some length, my critique of the interviewing procedure. That, of course, is all Paul had to hear.[1] "Well, Bob, it happens that we have another group coming in for a test. Will you show us how the interview should be done?" That was not a defensive-aggressive question, as you might mistakenly suppose it was. Rather, that was the founding Director of the Office of Radio Research (as of other university-linked organizations dedicated to social research) engaged in preliminary co-optation. I allow as how I will try my hand at it—and thus began my life with what would eventuate as the focussed group-interview.

I recall Paul having induced me to work on a distinctly preliminary analysis of those interview materials during the next days, the weekend. The report was in the Office of Facts and Figures within a week. That was in November 1941. Then came December 7th, and the war which held little nationalistic meaning but much moral significance for many of us back then. Not very much later and for some time during the war, I found myself serving as the liaison research person between the Columbia group and what had been established by the United States Army in October of that year as the Research Branch of what was successively known as the Morale Division, then the Special Services Division, and finally as the Information and Education Division. (The movement toward euphemisms had plainly begun). The Research Branch was directed on its research (not administrative) side by the ingenious and practiced social researcher Sam Stouffer (who would eventually see to it that a distillation of the field studies

---

1. In his passion to get all problems he thought important solved, Paul made it an enduring practice to co-opt associates of every kind to work on them— students, of course, but also colleagues of varied stripe; young and old; near and far; social scientists, logicians, mathematicians, statisticians, and philosophers. This pattern of disinterested co-optation has been beautifully recaptured in print by two of our students from those ancient days of the 1940s and 50s: James S. Coleman (1980) and David L. Sills (1987).

conducted during World War II would appear in the form of the four volumes of *The American Soldier*.) [2]

For a time, I found myself interviewing groups of soldiers in Army camps about their responses to specific training films and so-called morale films—some of them designed by Frank Capra and other directors of that calibre. In the course of that experience and later in work at the Bureau of Applied Social Research (which had evolved from the Columbia Office of Radio Research) , there developed the set of procedures which came to be known as the focussed interview. As Sam Stouffer noted in his preface to volume 4, those procedures were not reported there because, by agreement with him and his associate Carl Hovland, they had been published several years before in the paper by Pat Kendall and myself (Merton and Kendall, 1946) .

As early as 1943, also, we were putting focussed interviews to use with individuals as well as groups. A prime case in point is the study of a "radio marathon," then a wholly new historical phenomenon, which promised to provide a "strategic research site" for investigating the collective behavior and social contexts of mass persuasion (Merton, Fiske, and Curtis, [1946] 1971) . During a period of 18 hours, the pops singer Kate Smith, widely perceived as a charismatic patriot-figure, spoke a series of prepared texts on sixty-five occasions, eliciting the then unprecedented total of $39 million in war-bond pledges. We conducted focussed interviews with 100 New Yorkers who had listened to part or, in some cases, to all [!] of the Smith broadcasts, both those listeners who had responded by pledging a war bond and those who had not. These interviews were conducted with listeners individually in their homes, not collectively in a radio studio. In the absence of the program analyzer to provide points of departure, the interviews were focussed upon the broadcast texts which we had

---

2. Samuel A. Stouffer et al., The American Soldier: Adjustment During Army Life; Samuel A. Stouffer et al., The American Soldier: Combat and Its Aftermath; Carl I. Hovland, Arthur A. Lumsdaine, and Fred D. Sheffield, Experiments on Mass Communication; Samuel A. Stouffer et al., Measurement and Prediction. Princeton: Princeton University Press, 1949.

subjected to an intensive content analysis. The resulting qualitative materials did much to help shape the interpretation of the quantitative data, based upon polling interviews with a representative sample of about a thousand New Yorkers. It was the focussed-interview data that led to identification of a public distrust related to a sense of anomie—in which "common values were being submerged in a welter of private interests seeking satisfaction by virtually any means which are effective" (p. 10). Analysis of these data led us also to a social phenomenon: "in place of a sense of *Gemeinschaft*—genuine community of values—there intrudes pseudo-*Gemeinschaft*— the feigning of personal concern with the other fellow in order to manipulate him the better" (p. 142); in still other words, "the mere pretense of common values in order to further private interests" (p. 144). (See also Merton, 1975:83; Cohen, 1975; Beniger, 1987.)

The focussed interview of individuals did not exhibit certain assets and liabilities of the focussed interview of small groupings. (I say "groupings" since these were not, of course, *groups* in the sociological sense of having a common identity or a continuing unity, shared norms, and goals.) Still, interaction among the members of such pro tem contrived groups evidently served to elicit the elaboration of responses just as it may have contaminated individual responses by making for observable convergence of them. Correlatively, the individual interviews based on prior content-analysis of the matters under examination clearly allowed for more intensive elucidation by each person while not providing for the introduction of new leads stimulated by others.

Years later, Harriet Zuckerman adapted and developed this tactic of interviews with individuals focussed on the prior analysis of "texts" in her study of an ultra-elite, Nobel laureates in science (Zuckerman, 1972, 1977: App. A). There, the content being analyzed in detail to provide foci for the interview was of course far more complex and wide-ranging than in the studies of mass-communication behavior. It involved, for example, identifying hypothetically key events and sequences in the biographies of the laureates, provisional identification of their sociometric networks at various phases of their careers, the spotting of their successes and failures in research, and patterned sequences identified in their bibliographies. As Zuckerman noted, this was a kind of "focussed interview," one that provides for analysis and interpretation rather than only for chronicle (as is typically the case with "oral histories").

In light of all this, the reader will not be surprised to learn that, at least in its bold outlines, the disciplined use of focus-group data has an amiable congruence with what we were trying to do with the focussed interview back then. However, certain features of the *uses* of focus-group materials nowadays seem to contrast strongly with the ways in which we had been making use of focussed-interview materials. I have referred to my work with Sam Stouffer and the Research Branch which involved focussed group-interviews. That work was in conjunction with Carl Hovland, who headed up the Experimental Section of the Research Branch. Carl, who was on leave from Yale during the war, was possibly the most accomplished psychologist ever to work on the effects of social communication; he died in 1961 at the age of 48 but is remembered admiringly and affectionately by those of us who knew him well. Carl designed and directed the controlled experiments on the responses of soldiers to those training and "morale" films. One would think that the experimental use of test and control groups would be taken to provide a sufficient design for identifying the effects of the films. But Carl wisely recognized that this was not so. It could not provide the specific qualitative information we were able to provide through our focussed interviews. That information moved beyond the *net effects* of "the films"—a most complex set of evocative stimuli—to identify, at least provisionally, the elements and configurations of that complex experience which might have led to those effects. The quantitative experimental design enabled one to determine the aggregate effects but provided no clues to *what it was about the film's content* that might have produced the observed effects. The focussed interview was designed to provide such materials—it identified, provisionally and subject to checks through further quantitative experimental research, the aspects of situational experience leading to the observed outcomes. This is so in investigating a particular concrete experience, as in the case of responses to a particular film or radio program, or a recurrent experience, which, I take it, is often the research focus of focus-group research these days.

Our qualitative adjuncts to the experimental design soon convinced that brilliant designer of experiments Carl Hovland that both kinds of data were required for sound conclusions. The rigor of the controlled experiment had its costs since it meant giving up access to the phenomenological aspects of the real-life experience and invited mistaken inferences about the sources of that experienced response; the qualitative detail provided by the focussed group-interview in turn had its costs since it could lead only to new hypotheses about the sources and character of the response, which in turn required further quantitative or, in this case, further experimental research to test the hypotheses.

I gather that much focus-group research today as a growing type of market research does not involve this composite of both qualitative and quantitative inquiry. One gains the impression that focus-group research is sometimes being mercilessly misused as quick-and-easy claims for the validity of the research are not subjected to further, often quantitative test. Perhaps the pressures of the marketplace for quick-and-easy—possibly, for quick and relatively inexpensive—research make for this misuse of focus groups. That misuse—the term seems less harsh than "abuse"—consists in taking merely plausible interpretations deriving from qualitative group interviews and treating them as though they had been shown to be reliably valid for gauging the *distributions* of response.

Shannon's fundamental theory of communication reminds us that calculated redundancy has its uses by enlarging the probability that the message will get through. So I say redundantly and emphatically that, for us, qualitative focussed group-interviews were taken as sources of new ideas and new hypotheses, not as demonstrated findings with regard to the extent and distribution of the provisionally identified qualitative patterns of response. Those ideas and hypotheses had to be checked out by further survey research (or in the case of the Research Branch studies, by further experimental research). The point is that limited qualitative research cannot in principle deal with the distribution and extent of tentatively identified patterns. (Medicine discovered some time ago that clinical observations were no substitute for epidemiological investigation.) I can report that some of the hypotheses derived from focussed interviews during our collaborative work with Carl Hovland did *not* check out upon further inquiry. The point is, of course, that there is no way of knowing in advance of further systematic research which plausible interpretations (hypotheses) will pan out and which will not.

As to the historical relationship between the focussed interview and the current use of focus groups, I believe that while there are both continuities and discontinuities, there is rather more intellectual continuity than explicitly recognized historical continuity. After all, *The Focused Interview* sold only a few thousand copies, for the most part in the 1950s, I believe, and then went out of print. We have no evidence on the distribution of those copies—say, as between academics and market researchers. Looking into files, which over the years have proved to be a continuing source of serendipitous[3] and therefore surprising finds, I discover a long-forgotten letter in

---

3. In a printed transcript of my AAPOR talk (Merton, 1987b) I referred to an unpublished monograph by Robert K. Merton and Elinor Barber (1958) which treats the social and cultural contexts of the coinage of the word *serendipity* in the 18th century; the climate of relevant opinion in which it first saw print in the 19th; the diverse social circles of litterateurs, physical and social scientists, engineers, lexicographers, and historians into which it diffused; the changes of meaning undergone in the course of diffusion, and the ideological uses to which it has been variously put. I rather doubt that the diffusion of the focussed interview is ready for a comparable analysis.

the mid-1970s. It testifies that there was some direct and identifiable continuity which was then recognized by research
people in the world of commerce.

Benson & Benson, Inc.
P.O. Box 269
Princeton, N.J. 08540
June 17, 1976

Professor Robert K. Merton
Fayerweather Hall
Columbia University
New York, N.Y. 10027

Dear Professor Merton:

Over the years we have derived considerable use from our
copy of the second edition of *The Focussed Interview—A
Manual*. As you undoubtedly are aware, focussed group interviewing has become widespread in commercial circles and is
eliciting interest in the academic and non-profit research
sectors. Oddly enough, little has been written on the subject
in systematic fashion, and, in nearly every case, that which
has apparently should not have been. We have urged other
researchers to refer to the *Manual*, but invariably have been
told that copies simply are not to be found. In other words, we
apparently possess one of the last known copies of the *Manual*,
and, understandably, are reluctant to lend it out.

Now, we are starting to receive queries for Xerox copies.

Our copy carries no copyright and the Introduction suggests the report is in the public domain.

We would like to reprint the manual and offer it for sale
to interested researchers at about $10–$12 per copy, plus post-
age. We think it is only fair that we consult you on this first.
We would propose to offer the authors a 15% royalty on each
copy sold. Payment would be made semi-annually. . . .

Sincerely,
Robert Bezilla
Executive Vice President

Now, like a longtime qualitative researcher, I want to examine the part of this document which testified to continuity between academe and the marketplace. Note that it begins by referring to "our copy of . . . *The Focussed Interview—A Manual*." That must refer to the second mimeographed edition put out by the Columbia Bureau of Applied Social Research rather than the far more widely circulated letterpress edition published by The Free Press in 1956. This I infer from the spelling of the word *Focussed* in the title, a spelling I have always preferred and therefore adopted in the two Bureau editions but one which The Free Press (as before it, the editor of the *American Journal of Sociology*) had unwarrantably but forcibly diminished to *Focused*. Thus, the two-essed *Focussed* serves as a marker of the earlier editions. Note too that by 1976, the executive vice president of Benson & Benson is reporting that "focussed [n.b.] group interviewing has become widespread in commercial circles and is eliciting interest in the academic and non-profit sectors." If his impression was sound, this suggests—somewhat to my startle now and perhaps back in 1976—that the pattern of focussed group-interviewing had expanded to the point of eliciting enlarged interest in the academic world where it had originated. Not to continue with a line-by-line gloss, I remark only on the decency of Robert Bezilla, then of Benson & Benson, in suggesting a royalty to the authors should he be allowed to reprint the manual; this, mind you, even though he (mistakenly) assumed that the work was in the public domain.

That is one indication of direct continuity between academia and the marketplace. I gather that during the passage from Morningside Heights to Madison Avenue the focussed interview has undergone some sea changes of the kind I've been in a position only to hint at: the quick would-be conversion of new plausible insights into demonstrable gospel truths. I am not really qualified to speak to this point since I've seen next to nothing of current focus-group research at close range. But I note the following observation by Leo Bogart (1984:82) :

In the 1970s, another type of qualitative research rapidly moved to the forefront: the so-called focus group interview in which a half-dozen to a dozen people are assembled and engaged in a discussion. (The term *focus group* is a barbarism that confused sociologist Robert K. Merton's technique of an unstructured but "focused" interview—in which a skillful interrogator keeps the respondent's attention from wandering off the subject at hand—and the traditional sociological technique of talking to a homogenous or related group of people who stimulate each other under the interviewer's guidance.[4]) A group interview can be conducted with little more expense than an intensive interview with one individual, but since everyone in the group gets counted, a respectable number of respondents can be totted up in the sample.

The most beguiling aspect of focus groups is that they can be observed in action by clients and creative people hidden behind a one-way mirror. Thus, the planners and executors of advertising can be made to feel that they are themselves privy to the innermost revelations of the consuming public. They *know* what consumers think of the product, the competition, and the advertising, having heard it at first hand. The trouble is that people who can be enticed into a research laboratory do not always represent a true cross-section of potential customers. A cadre of professional respondents are always ready to volunteer, and loud-mouths can dominate and sway the discussion. While useful and provocative ideas emerge from groups just as they do from individual qualitative interviews, it is dangerous to accept them without corroboration from larger-scale survey research.

So much for critical observations on some present-day practices in focus-group research. Now back for a few moments to the archives. Roaming through my files of that full generation ago—recall what Ortega y Gasset, Karl Mannheim, and Julián Marías had to say about the social reality and dynamics of generations—I have come upon a long-forgotten letter to Jeremiah Kaplan, the founding president of The Free Press, telling how

---

4. Paul F. Lazarsfeld and Frank Stanton first combined these techniques in the radio Program Analyzer. Groups of people pressed buttons to record their moment-by-moment responses to what they heard. The interviewer, examining the tape, questioned them as to why they reacted as they did. CBS still uses this technique to evaluate television programs.

the mimeographed editions of *The Focussed Interview* came to be transformed into the printed edition.

[Mr. Jeremiah Kaplan
The Free Press]
8 August 1955

Dear Jerry,

. . . The news of the moment is this: I have set myself a quota, during these comfortable vacation-days, of so many pages a day for rewriting the Focused Interview. Now that a week has gone by and I am still on schedule, I am quite confident that it will be completed by the time I return. Since my secretary is away next week, there will be a little delay in typing this new version but the ms. will definitely be ready for the printer by the end of the month. . . .

Item 1: This is a complete *re-writing;* scarcely five sentences in a chapter remain intact. Nevertheless it is not, in any significant sense, a new *edition;* there is next to nothing by way of new material (except for a little based on focused interviews on the diaries of medical students) and little by way of new ideas. I've tried only to eliminate the worst horrors of exposition in the earlier printings and, for the rest, to make it clear, if not fascinating. It seems to me, therefore, that it should not be designated as a new edition, but as the Third Re-printing (rewritten) , so that no excessive claims seem to be implied. I hope you agree. (I'll explain the nature of the rewriting in the preface.)

Item 2: As you know, this is a short book—it will run to about 230 ms. pages (including about 25 single-spaced pages of an analytical table of contents which was found useful in the Bureau 'editions') . I wouldn't like to have the book be too expensive: it is all straight text, no tables or charts, and should be easy to set in type. At the same time, I hope that Sid can design it so that it isn't too crowded. Can you let me have your thinking on price and design? . . .

Yours,
Bob

As can be seen, by the mid-1950s the essential concept of the focussed interview and its basic procedures with their stated rationales had become stabilized. Indeed, these did not evolve further at the Columbia Bureau. So it was that this interlinear rewriting of the Manual became the version that could diffuse and evidently did diffuse into various research sectors, notably it seems into the sector of market research.

That particular pathway of diffusion into the marketplace was neither intended nor, as I recall, anticipated. Speaking for myself, I thought of the focussed interview as a generic research technique, one that could be and would be applied in every sphere of human behavior and experience, rather than largely confined to matters of interest in market research. As for the actual paths of diffusion taken by the focussed interview, no case study of that diffusion has been made. Perhaps a study utilizing the now available resources of citation analysis coupled with interview or questionnaire inquiries among representative samples of different populations of social researchers would provide some understanding of the extent and directions of that diffusion of a modest, delimited, and readily identifiable innovation as well as the kinds and determinants of diverse kinds of changes in it as it spread to one or another research sector. Not that the diffusion of this technique warrants such a study because of its research importance but only because it seems to have some of the elements of a strategic research site[5] for investigation of the diffusion of intellectual innovations—a subject of deep interest in the Columbia Bureau of Applied Social Research back in the 1960s, as some may recall from the path-breaking study by James Coleman, Elihu Katz, and Herbert Menzel (1966). Lately that interest has been brilliantly renewed on Morningside Heights by Ronald S. Burt (1987) in his reanalysis of the Coleman-Katz-Menzel data.

---

5. The concept of strategic research site is elucidated somewhat in Merton, 1987a.

So much for an excursion into the serious, systematic study of the diffusion of innovations. Here I can only turn to the archives which once again yield a bit of pertinent evidence— evidence which bears witness that the focussed interview was not confined to academe or the marketplace but, at least once, found its way into the sphere of religion:

> Board of Education
> The United Methodist Church
> Division of the Local Church
> September 18, 1969

Dr. Robert K. Merton
Department of Sociology
Columbia University
New York, New York 10027

Dear Dr. Merton:

We are conducting a major study of the state of the church school of The United Methodist Church and would like to make use of the focused interview technique which you have described in the book by that title.

I am having difficulty locating additional copies of the book and am wondering if you could direct me to a supplier from whom we might purchase copies for use in our training sessions. Up to this time the only copies we have been able to discover are those which are in several libraries.

Your help in this matter will be greatly appreciated.

> Cordially yours,
> Warren J. Hartman

Now to a few more bits of documentary evidence on the continuity from the focussed interview as a mode of social and psychological inquiry to the focus group. I turn to the fairly recent past for a few qualitative indicators of that continuity. In 1976, precisely thirty years after Pat Kendall's and my first publication on the focussed interview, an introduction in a book entitled *Qualitative Research in Marketing* by Danny Bellenger, Kenneth Bernhardt, and Jack Goldstrucker (published by the American Marketing Association) virtually begins by reporting that "Merton, Fiske, and Kendall distinguish the focus group as following these criteria" and then proceeds to quote the paragraph on "The Nature of the Focused Interview" that opens our book. Here one may note a diagnostic conflating of the focussed interview and the focus group, at least a terminological conflation. We never used the term "focus group"—at least, not as I recall—but apparently these authors on marketing research saw the focus group as so fully derivative as to have us setting down criteria for focus groups. To be sure, we repeatedly examine the values and limitations of using focussed interviews in groups rather than independently with later aggregated individuals and that might be a basic theme in the continuity-cum-change.

Recognition of the accent on that theme is found in a fairly recent article published in *Information Technology and Libraries* (December 1983). Introducing a research program for library users and on-line public access catalogs (OPACS), it has occasion to refer to "focused-group interviews" and goes on to say (p. 381) that "complete descriptions of the focused-group interview method and analysis are given in Merton, Fiske and Kendall's manual on the method."

Earlier I ventured the impression that there was more "intellectual continuity" between the focussed interview and focus groups than "explicitly recognized historical continuity." The distinction between the two kinds of continuity is one that has long seemed basic to me in trying to understand patterns in the historical transmission of knowledge. For in the course of time, ideas which are taken up and utilized or developed become so much a part of current knowledge, both explicit and tacit, that their sources and consequently the lines of intellectual continuity get increasingly lost to view. I have identified this phenomenon in the transmission of knowledge as "obliteration by incorporation (OBI)": "the obliteration of the sources of ideas, methods, or findings by their incorporation in currently accepted knowledge."[6] At the outset, the source of a particular idea or method is known and identified

---

6. The phenomenon of OBI is noted in Merton, 1968, and in other writings since. This summary is drawn from Merton, 1979; see also Garfield, 1977.

by those who make use of it. In due course, however, users and consequently transmitters of that knowledge who are thoroughly familiar with its origins come to assume that this is also true of their readers. Preferring not to be obvious or to insult their reader's assumed knowledgeability, they no longer refer to the *original* source. And since, in all innocence, many of us tend to attribute a significant idea, method, or formulation to the author who introduced us to it, the equally innocent transmitter sometimes becomes identified as the originator. Thus it is that in the successive transmission of knowledge, repeated use of it may erase all but the immediately antecedent "source," thus producing what I described in *On the Shoulders of Giants* (Merton, 1965:218–219ff.) as a historical palimpsest (or palimpsestic syndrome) in which the *original* source is not only obliterated but replaced by the intermediary between source and recipient of that knowledge.

Without doing the requisite research, I cannot presume to say how much of the seeming discontinuity between the focussed interview and its modified version in the form of focus groups is actually another instance of obliteration by incorporation. But that some OBI has occurred can be inferred from an article by two professors of sociology at the University of California–Riverside, David L. Morgan and Margaret T. Spanish (1984), which describes "focus groups" as "a relatively new research tool" (p. 253). If the focussed interview has experienced even occasional obliteration by incorporation in the originating field of sociology, one is inclined to suppose that it is all the more (a fortiori) likely to have occurred in other fields into which it had diffused.

And now a final word, stemming once again from the marketplace, but one which, much to my pleasure, recognizes that the focussed interview is not at all confined to market research. Indeed, in light of its use by religious and other eleemosynary institutions, it might even be described as ecumenical. But perhaps more telling is a review of *The Focused Interview* appearing in the October 1956 issue of *The Journal of Marketing.* Understandably, the review is oriented to its probable readers in remarking that the book "should be of particular value to the student and practitioner of marketing research." Good enough; more qualitative evidence of diffusion from academe to the marketplace. But much more in point for the original concept of the focussed interview as a generic rather than substantively restricted research tool is the concluding declaration in the review that "This manual should be read by those who are attempting to understand the problems involved in subjective or motivation research in whatever field it may lie." Precisely so. Useful for marketing research, to be sure, but not only for marketing research. Rather, a set of procedures for the collection and analysis of qualitative data that may help us gain an enlarged sociological and psychological understanding in whatsoever sphere of human experience.

Robert K. Merton

References

Beniger, James R. (1987)
"Personalization of mass media and the growth of pseudo-community." *Communication Research* 14:352–371.

Bogart, Leo (1984)
Strategy in Advertising. 2d ed. Chicago: Crain Books.

Burt, Ronald S. (1987)
"Social contagion and innovation: Cohesion versus structural equivalence." *American Journal of Sociology* 92:1287–1335.

Cohen, Harry (1975)
"Pseudo- *Gemeinschaft*: A problem of modern society." *Western Sociological Review* 5:35–46.

Coleman, James S. (1980)
"Paul F. Lazarsfeld: The substance and style of his work." Pp. 153–174 in Robert K. Merton and Matilda White Riley (eds.), *Sociological Traditions from Generation to Generation:*

Glimpses of the American Experience. Norwood, NJ: Ablex Publishing Corp.

Coleman, James S., Elihu Katz, and Herbert Menzel (1966)
Medical Innovation: A Diffusion Study. Indianapolis: Bobbs-Merrill.

De Lellio, Anna (1985)
"Intervista a Robert K. Merton: Le aspettative di durata." *Rassegna Italiana di Sociologia* 26:3–26.

Garfield, Eugene (1977)
"The 'obliteration phenomenon' in science—and the advantage of being obliterated!" Pp. 396–398 in Eugene Garfield, *Essays of an Information Scientist,* vol. 2. Philadelphia: ISI Press.

Hunt, Morton (1961)
" 'How does it come to be so?': A profile of Robert K. Merton." *The New Yorker,* January 28.

Lazarsfeld, Paul F. (1975)
"Working with Merton." Pp. 36–66 in Lewis A. Coser (ed.), *The Idea of Social Structure.* New York: Harcourt Brace Jovanovich.

Merton, Robert K. [1965] (1985)
On the Shoulders of Giants. New York: Harcourt Brace Jovanovich.

——— (1968)
Social Theory and Social Structure. New York: Free Press.

——— (1975)
"On the origins of the term: pseudo-*Gemeinschaft.*" *Western Sociological Review* 6:83.

——— (1979)
Foreword to Eugene Garfield, *Citation Indexing: Its Theory and Application in Science, Technology, and Humanities.* New York: John Wiley.

——— (1987a)
"Three fragments from a sociologist's notebook: Establishing the phenomenon, specified ignorance, and strategic research materials." *Annual Review of Sociology* 13:1–28.

——— (1987b)
"The focussed interview and focus groups: Continuities and discontinuities." *Public Opinion Quarterly* 51:550–566.

Merton, Robert K., and Elinor Barber (1958)
"The travels and adventures of serendipity: A study in historical semantics and the sociology of science." Manuscript.

Merton, Robert K., with Marjorie Fiske and Alberta Curtis [1946] (1971)
Mass Persuasion. New York: Harper and Bros. Reprint, Westport, CT: Greenwood Press.

Merton, Robert K., Marjorie Fiske, and Patricia L. Kendall [1956] (1990)
The Focused Interview. New York: Free Press.

Merton, Robert K., and Patricia L. Kendall (1946)
"The focused interview." *American Journal of Sociology* 51: 541–557.

Morgan, David L., and Margaret T. Spanish (1984)
"Focus groups: A new tool for qualitative research." *Qualitative Sociology* 7:253–270.

Sills, David L. (1987)
"Paul F. Lazarsfeld, 1901–1976: A biographical memoir." Pp. 251–282 in *National Academy of Sciences, Biographical Memoirs*. Washington: The National Academy Press.

Zuckerman, Harriet (1972)
"Interviewing an ultra-elite." *Public Opinion Quarterly* 36: 159–175.

————— (1977)
Scientific Elite: Nobel Laureates in the United States. New York: Free Press.

The Focused Interview

CHAPTER I

Purposes and Criteria

Nature of the Focused Interview

The focused interview differs in several respects from other types of research interview which might appear similar at first glance. In broad outline, its distinguishing characteristics are as follows. First of all, the persons interviewed are known to have been involved in *a particular situation:* they have seen a film, heard a radio program, read a pamphlet, article or book, taken part in a psychological experiment or in an uncontrolled, but observed, social situation (for example, a political rally, a ritual or a riot). Secondly, the hypothetically significant elements, patterns, processes and total structure of this situation have been provisionally analyzed by the social scientist. Through this *content or situational analysis,* he has arrived at a set of hypotheses concerning the consequences of determinate aspects of the situation for those involved in it. On the basis of this analysis, he takes the third step of developing an *interview guide,* setting forth the major areas of inquiry and the hypotheses which provide criteria of relevance for the data to be obtained in the interview. Fourth and finally, the interview is focused on the subjective experiences of persons exposed to the pre-analyzed situation in an effort to ascertain *their definitions of the situation.* The array of reported responses to the situation helps

(3)

test hypotheses and, to the extent that it includes unanticipated responses, gives rise to fresh hypotheses for more systematic and rigorous investigation.

From this synopsis it will be seen that a distinctive prerequisite of the focused interview is a prior analysis of the
situation in which subjects have been involved. Such fore-
knowledge of the situation is clearly at an optimum in the
case of experimentally contrived situations, although it can
be acquired also in uncontrolled, but observed, situations.
Equipped in advance with an analysis of the situation, the
interviewer can readily distinguish the objective facts of the
case from the subjective definitions of the situation. He is
thus alerted to the patterns of selective response. Through
his familiarity with the objective situation, the interviewer
is better prepared to recognize symbolic or functional
silences, distortions, avoidances, or blockings and is, consequently, better prepared to explore their implications. The
prior analysis thus helps him to detect and to explore private
logics, symbolism and spheres of tension. It helps him gauge
the importance of what is not being said, as well as of what
is being said, in successive stages of the interview.

Finally, prior content or situational analysis facilitates the
flow of concrete and detailed reporting of responses. Summary generalizations by the interviewee mean that he is
presenting, not the raw data for interpretation, but the
interpretation itself. It is not enough to learn that an interviewee regarded a situation as "unpleasant" or "anxiety-pro-
voking" or "stimulating"—summary judgments which are
properly suspect and, moreover, consistent with a variety of
interpretations. The aim is to discover more precisely what
"unpleasant" denotes in this context, which concrete feelings
were called into play, which personal associations came to
mind. Furthermore, when subjects are led to describe their
reactions in great detail, there is less prospect that they will,
intentionally or unwittingly, conceal the actual character of
their responses.

The interviewer who has previously analyzed the situation on which the interview focuses is in a peculiarly advantageous position to elicit such detail. In the usual depth interview, one can encourage informants to reminisce about their experiences. In the focused interview, the interviewer can play a more active role; he can introduce more explicit verbal cues to the stimulus situation or even *re-present* it, as we shall see. In either case, this ordinarily activates a concrete report of responses by interviewees.

Uses of the Focused Interview

The focused interview was initially developed to meet certain problems growing out of communications research and propaganda analysis. The outlines of such problems appear in detailed case studies by Dr. Herta Herzog, dealing with the gratification found by listeners in various types of radio programs.[1] With the sharpening of objectives, research interest centered on the analysis of responses to particular pamphlets, radio programs, and motion pictures. During the war, Dr. Herzog and the senior author of this manual were assigned by several war agencies to study the social and psychological effects of specific efforts to build morale. In the course of this work, the focused interview was progressively developed to a relatively standardized form.

In the beginning, the primary, though not the exclusive, purpose of the focused interview was to provide some basis for *interpreting* statistically significant effects of mass communications. But, in general, *experimental studies of effects,* and inquiries into patterned definitions of social situations might well profit by the use of focused interviews in research. The character of such applications can be briefly illustrated

---

1. "What Do We Really Know about Daytime Serial Listeners?," in Paul F. Lazarsfeld and Frank N. Stanton (eds.), *Radio Research, 1942-43* (New York: Duell, Sloan and Pearce, 1944).

by examining the role of the focused interview at four distinct points:

1. specifying the effective stimulus;
2. interpreting discrepancies between anticipated and actual effects;
3. interpreting discrepancies between prevailing effects and effects among subgroups—"deviant cases";
4. interpreting processes involved in experimentally induced effects.

1. Experimental studies of effect face the problem of what might be called the *specification of the stimulus, i.e.,* determining which x or patterns of x's in the total stimulus situation led to the observed effects. But, largely because of the practical difficulties which it entails, this requirement is often not satisfied in psychological or sociological experiments. Instead, a relatively undifferentiated complex of factors—such as "emotional appeals," "competitive incentives," and "political propaganda"—is regarded as "the" experimental variable. This would be comparable to the statement that "living in the tropics is a cause of higher rates of malaria"; it is true but unspecific. However crude they may be at the outset, procedures must be devised to detect the causally significant aspects of the total stimulus situation. Thus Gosnell conducted an ingenious experiment on the "stimulation of voting," in which experimental groups of residents in twelve districts in Chicago were sent "individual nonpartisan appeals" to register and vote.[2] Roughly equivalent control groups did not receive this literature. It was found that the experimental groups responded by a significantly higher proportion of registration and voting. But what does this result demonstrate? Was it the nonpartisan character of the circulars, the explicit nature of the instructions which they contained, the particular symbols and appeals utilized in the

---

2. Harold F. Gosnell, *Getting Out the Vote: An Experiment in the Stimulation of Voting* (Chicago: University of Chicago Press, 1927).

notices, or what? In short, to use Gosnell's own phrasing, what were "the particular stimuli being tested"?

According to the ideal experimental design, such questions would, of course, be answered by a series of successive experiments, which test the effects of each pattern of putative causes. In practice not only does the use of this procedure in social experimentation involve prohibitive problems of cost, labor, and administration; it also assumes that the experimenter has managed to detect the pertinent aspects of the total stimulus pattern. The focused interview provides a useful near-substitute for such a series of experiments; for, despite great sacrifices in scientific exactitude, it enables the experimenter to arrive at plausible hypotheses concerning the significant items to which subjects responded. Through interviews focused on this problem, Gosnell, for example, could probably have arrived at testable hypotheses about the elements in his several types of "nonpartisan" materials which proved effective for different segments of his experimental group.[3] Such a procedure provides an approximate solution for problems[4] heretofore consigned to the realm of

---

3. Significantly enough, Gosnell did interview citizens in several election districts who received notices. However, he apparently did not focus the interviews in such fashion as to enable him to determine the significant phases of the total stimulus pattern. See his summary remark that "interviews . . . brought out the fact that [the notices] had been read with interest and that they had aroused considerable curiosity." And note his speculation that "part of the effect [of the mail canvass] may have been due to the novelty of the appeal" (*op. cit.*, pp. 29, 71). Properly oriented focused interviews would have enabled him to detect the points of "interest," the ineffectual aspects of the notices, and differences in response by different types of citizens.

4. The same problem arises in a more complicated and difficult form when the experimental situation is not a limited event but an elaborate complex of experiences. Thus Chapin studied the gains in social participation which can be attributed "to the effects of living in the [public] housing project." As he recognized, "improved housing" is an unanalyzed "experimental" situation: managerial policies, increased leisure, architectural provision for group meetings, and a host of other items are varying elements of the program of "improved housing." (See F. S. Chapin, "An Experiment on the Social Effects of Good Housing," *American Sociological Review*, 5 [1940], 868-79.)

the unknown or the speculative, and provides for further and more sharply focused experiments.

2. There is also the necessity for *interpreting* the effects which are found to occur. Quite frequently, for example, the experimenter will note a *discrepancy* between the observed effects and those anticipated on the basis of other findings or previously formulated theories. Or, again, he may find that one subgroup in his experimental population exhibits effects which differ in degree or direction from those observed among other parts of the population. Unless the research is to remain a compendium of unintegrated empirical findings, some effort must be made to interpret such "contradictory" results. But the difficulty here is that of selecting among the wide range of *post factum* interpretations of the deviant findings. The focused interview provides a tool for this purpose. For example:

> Rosenthal's study of the effect of "pro-radical" motion-picture propaganda on the socioeconomic attitudes of college students provides an instance of *discrepancy between anticipated and actual effects*.[5] He found that a larger proportion of subjects agreed with the statement "radicals are enemies of society" *after* they had seen the film. As is usually the case when seemingly paradoxical results are obtained, this called forth an "explanation": "This negative effect of the propaganda was probably due to the many scenes of radical orators, marchers, and demonstrators."

Clearly *ad hoc* in nature, this "interpretation" is little more than speculation; but it is the type of speculation which the focused interview is particularly suited to examine, correct, and develop. Such interviews would have indicated how the audience actually responded to the "orators, marchers, and demonstrators"; the author's conjecture would have been recast into theoretical terms and either confirmed or refuted. (As we shall see, the focused interview has, in fact, been used

5. Solomon P. Rosenthal, "Change of Socioeconomic Attitudes under Radical Motion Picture Propaganda," *Archives of Psychology,* No. 166 (1934).

to locate the probable source of such "boomerang effects" in film, radio, pamphlet, and cartoon propaganda.) [6]

In a somewhat similar experiment, Peterson and Thurstone found an unexpectedly small change in attitudes among high-school students who had seen a pacifist film.[7] The investigators held it ". . . probable that the picture, 'Journey's End,' is too sophisticated in its propaganda for high school children."

Once again, the plausibility of a *post factum* interpretation would have been enhanced, and entirely different hypotheses would have been developed had they conducted a focused interview.[8] How did the children conceive the film? To what did they primarily respond? Answers to these and similar questions would yield the kind of data needed to interpret the unanticipated result.

3. We may turn again to Gosnell's study to illustrate the tendency toward *ad hoc* interpretations of *discrepancies between prevailing effects and effects among subgroups* ("deviant cases") and the place of focused interviews in avoiding them.

Gosnell found that, in general, a larger proportion of citizens registered or voted in response to a notice "of a hortatory character, containing a cartoon and several slogans" than in response to a "factual" notice, which merely called attention to voting regulations. But he found a series of "exceptions," which invited a medley of *ad hoc* hypotheses. In a predominantly German election district,

---

6. Paul F. Lazarsfeld and Robert K. Merton, "Studies in Radio and Film Propaganda," *Transactions of the New York Academy of Sciences, Series II,* 6 (1943), 58-79; Robert K. Merton and Patricia Kendall, "The Boomerang Effect—Problems of the Health and Welfare Publicist," *Channels* (National Publicity Council), XXI (1944); and Paul F. Lazarsfeld and Patricia Kendall, "The Listener Talks Back," in *Radio in Health Education* (prepared under the auspices of the New York Academy of Medicine) (New York: Columbia University Press, 1945).

7. Ruth C. Peterson and L. L. Thurstone, *Motion Pictures and the Social Attitudes of Children* (New York: Macmillan Co., 1933).

8. On the problems of *post factum* interpretations see R. K. Merton, "Sociological Theory," *American Journal of Sociology,* 50 (1945), esp. 467-69.

the factual notice had a greater effect than the "cartoon notice"—a finding which at once led Gosnell to the supposition that "the word 'slacker' on the cartoon notice probably revived war memories and therefore failed to arouse interest in voting." In Czech and Italian districts the factual notices also proved more effective; but in these instances Gosnell advances quite another interpretation: "the information cards were more effective than the cartoon notices probably because they were printed in Czech [and Italian, respectively] whereas the cartoon notices were printed in English." And yet in a Polish district the factual notice, although printed in Polish, was slightly *less* effective than the cartoon notice.[9]

In short, lacking supplementary interviews focused on the problem of deviant group responses, the investigator found himself drawn into a series of self-generated conjectures instead of deriving tentative interpretations from interviewees' reports of actual experience. This characteristic of the Gosnell experiment, properly assessed by Catlin as an exceptionally well-planned study, is, *a fortiori,* found in a host of social and psychological experiments.

4. Even brief introspective interviews as a supplement to experimentation have proved useful for discerning *processes involved in experimentally induced effects.* Thus Zeigarnik, in her well-known experiment on memory and interrupted tasks, was confronted with the result that in some cases interrupted tasks were often forgotten, a finding at odds with her modal findings and her initial theory.[10] Interviews with subjects exhibiting this "discrepant" behavior revealed that the uncompleted tasks which had been forgotten were experienced as failures and, therefore, were subjectively "completed." She was thus able to incorporate this seeming contradiction into her general theory. The value of such interpretative interviews is evidenced further in the fact that

---

9. *Op. cit.,* pp. 60, 64, 65, 67.

10. B. Zeigarnik, "Das Behalten erledigter und unerledigter Handlungen," *Psychologische Forschung,* 9 (1927), 1-85.

Zeigarnik's extended theory, derived from the interviews, inspired a series of additional experiments by Rosenzweig, who, in part, focused on the very hypotheses which emerged from her interview data.

> Rosenzweig found experimentally that many subjects recalled a larger percentage of their successes in tasks assigned them than of their failures.[11] Interviews disclosed that this "objective experimental result" was bound up with the personal symbolism which tasks assumed for different subjects. For example, one subject reported that a needed scholarship depended "upon her receiving a superior grade in the psychology course from which she had been recruited for this experiment. Throughout the test her mind dwelt upon the lecturer in this course: 'All I thought of during the experiment was that it was an intelligence test and that he [the lecturer] would see the results. I saw his name always before me.' "

Such supplementary data invited the hypothesis of repression to interpret the results.

This brief review is perhaps sufficient to suggest the functions of the focused interview as an adjunct to experimental inquiry, as well as to studies of responses to situations encountered in everyday life.

Criteria of the Effective Focused Interview

In order to achieve one or more of these several functions, the interviewer must develop the practice of continuously assessing the interview as it is in process. By drawing upon a large number of interview transcripts, in which the questions and remarks of the interviewer as well as the responses of interviewees have been recorded, we have evolved a set of criteria which seem to distinguish between productive and unproductive interview materials.

---

11. Saul Rosenzweig, "The Experimental Study of Repression," in H. A. Murray, (ed.) , *Explorations in Personality* (New York: Oxford University Press, 1938) , pp. 472-90.

Briefly stated, these are:

1. *Range.* The interview should enable interviewees to maximize the reported range of evocative elements and patterns in the stimulus situation as well as the range of responses.
2. *Specificity.* The interview should elicit highly specific reports of the aspects of the stimulus situation to which interviewees have responded.
3. *Depth.* The interview should help interviewees to describe the affective, cognitive and evaluative meanings of the situation and the degree of their involvement in it.
4. *Personal context.* The interview should bring out the attributes and prior experience of interviewees which endow the situation with these distinctive meanings.

These criteria are interrelated: *they are merely different dimensions of the same concrete body of interview material.* Reports can be classified according to each of these dimensions: they may be wide-ranging or narrowly restricted; highly specific or general and diffuse; profoundly self-revealing or superficial; and indicative of the personal context of response or wholly unrelated to the status, values and past experience of the individual. Although these criteria are merely different aspects of the same data, it is useful to examine them separately, in order to provide the interviewer with guide-lines for appraising the flow of the interview and for adapting his techniques accordingly.

With respect to each of these criteria, there is an array of more or less standardized procedures which have been found reasonably effective. *Only a few of these procedures do not lend themselves to more than one purpose.* In the following chapters, we shall examine the major function served by each technique and merely allude to its subsidiary functions.

NONDIRECTION

As is generally recognized, one of the principal reasons for the use of interviews rather than questionnaires is to uncover a diversity of relevant responses, whether or not these have been anticipated by the inquirer. There would be little point in using the interview at all, if it simply resolved itself into a fixed list of stock questions put by the interviewer. For this would abandon a distinctive merit of the interview in comparison with the questionnaire: the give-and-take which helps the interviewee decode and report the meanings which a situation held for him. It would mean the loss of that collaboration which encourages the interviewee to continue his self-exploration of an experience until some measure of clarity is attained.

The maintenance of spontaneity of report is not, of course, distinctive of the focused interview; on the contrary, it is one of the characteristics which it shares with nondirective interviews generally. Since nondirective procedures for encouraging spontaneity of report are not singled out for systematic discussion later in this book, it may be useful to summarize, at this point, the gist of our thinking about them.

The value of a nondirective approach to interviewing has become increasingly recognized, notably since the work of Carl Rogers and of Roethlisberger and Dickson.[12] It gives the interviewee an opportunity to express himself about matters of central significance to him rather than those presumed to be important by the interviewer.[13] That is, in contrast to the polling approach, it uncovers what is on the interviewee's mind rather than his opinion of what is on the interviewer's mind. Furthermore, it allows his responses to be placed in

---

12. Carl R. Rogers, *Counseling and Psychotherapy* (New York: Houghton Mifflin Co., 1942), pp. 115-28; F. J. Roethlisberger and W. J. Dickson, *Management and the Worker* (Cambridge: Harvard University Press, 1938), Chap. XIII.

13. Thus meeting the objection raised by Stuart A. Rice: "A defect of the interview for the purposes of fact-finding in scientific research, then, is that the questioner *takes the lead.* That is, the subject plays a more or less passive role. Information or points of view of the highest value may not be disclosed because the direction given the interview by the questioner leads away from them. In short, data obtained from an interview are as likely to embody the preconceived ideas of the interviewer as the attitudes of the subject interviewed," (S. A. Rice [ed.], *Methods in Social Science* [Chicago: University of Chicago Press, 1931], p. 561).

their proper context rather than forced into a framework which the interviewer considers appropriate. And, finally, it ordinarily leads the interviewee to be more articulate and expressive than in the directed interview.[14]

Direction in interviewing is largely incompatible with eliciting *unanticipated* responses. Private definitions of the stimulus situation are rarely forthcoming when directive techniques are used. By their very nature, direct questions presuppose a certain amount of structuring by the interviewer. Direct questions, even though they are not "leading" in character, force subjects to focus their attention on items and issues to which they might not have responded on their own initiative. (This is a basic limitation of those questionnaires or schedules which provide no opportunity for subjects to express a lack of concern with items on which they are questioned.) For instance, a civilian group who had seen a documentary film dealing with the war in Italy were asked: "Did you feel proud or annoyed when you saw how the Americans were helping in the reconstruction of Naples?" A directed question of this type at once prejudices the possibility of determining how the interviewees had structured the film. The film might have been experienced impersonally as merely "interesting information." The question implies that Americans were actually taking part in the reconstruction, although, as was found in other interviews, some found the film vague on this point. Even had they recognized that Americans were engaged in reconstruction, they may have learned only from the question that others were also engaged in the same work. Their replies reflected some of these implications and suggestions which had colored their own interpretation of the film and ruled out the possibility of

---

14. Rogers (*op. cit.,* p. 122), reporting an unpublished study by E. H. Porter, states that in ten directive interviews, the interviewer talked nearly three times as much as the subject. In nine nondirective interviews, on the other hand, the interviewer talked only half as much as the subject.

indicating misapprehensions. A single direct question can inadvertently supply many biasing connotations.

Nondirective techniques sometimes prove ineffective in halting irrelevant and unproductive digressions, so that the interviewer seemingly has no alternative but to introduce a direct question. But in a focused interview the limits of relevance are largely self-defined for the interviewee by the concrete situation to which he has been exposed. Not only are digressions less likely to occur, but, when they do occur, they are more easily dealt with by nondirective references to the concrete situation. In other words, the focal character of the experience results in a maximum yield of pertinent data through nondirective procedures.

PROCEDURES

The interrelations of our criteria at once become evident when we observe that nondirection simultaneously serves to elicit depth, range, specificity and personal context of responses. Unstructured questions are intentionally couched in such terms that they invite subjects to refer to virtually any aspect of the stimulus situation or to report any of a range of responses. In answering a query of this type, the individual provides a crude guide to the comparative significance of various aspects of the situation.

In the focused interview, then, an unstructured question is one which does not fix attention on any specific aspect of the stimulus situation or of the response; it is, so to speak, a blank page to be filled in by the interviewee. But questions have varying degrees of structure. Several levels of structure can be distinguished as a guide to the interviewer.

1. *Unstructured question (stimulus and response free)*.
   What impressed you most in this film?
                    or
   What stood out especially in this conference?

   This type of query leads the interviewee, rather than the interviewer, to indicate the foci of attention. He has an entirely free choice. Not only is he given an opportunity to refer to any aspect of the stimulus pattern, but the phrases "impressed you" and "stood out" are sufficiently general to invite reports of quite varied types of responses.

2. *Semistructured question.*
   Type A: *Response structured, stimulus free.*
   What did you learn from this pamphlet which you hadn't known before?
   Type B: *Stimulus structured, response free.*
   How did you feel about the part describing Joe's discharge from the army as a psychoneurotic?

   There is obviously increased guidance by the interviewer in both types of query, but the informant still retains considerable freedom of reply. In Type A, although restricted to reports of newly acquired information, he is free to refer to any item in the pamphlet. In Type B, conversely, he is confined to one section of the document but is free to indicate the nature of his response.

3. *Structured question (stimulus and response structured).*
   Judging from the film, do you think that the German fighting equipment was better, as good as, or poorer than the equipment used by Americans?

   or

   As you listened to Chamberlain's speech, did you feel it was propagandistic or informative?

   Through questions of this type the interviewer assumes almost complete control of the interview. Not only does he single out items for comment, but he also suggests an *order of response* which he assumes was experienced. This leads to an oral questionnaire rather than a free interview.

Although the fully unstructured question is especially appropriate in the opening stages of the focused interview, where its productivity is at a peak, it is profitably used throughout the interview. In some instances it may be necessary for the interviewer to assume more control at later stages of the interview, if the criteria of specificity, range, depth and personal context are to be satisfied. But even in such cases, as we shall see, moderate rather than full direction is fruitful; questions should be partially rather than fully structured.

Objectives of the Manual

Now that we have reviewed the nature and purposes of the focused interview, it may be in order to indicate what we hope to accomplish in the chapters which follow. The preparation of a manual for interviewing presupposes some conception of the extent to which interviewing skills can be described and taught. We do not suppose that interviewing procedures can be so completely routinized that individual differences in aptitude are eliminated. It is clear that a fixed routine of mechanically applied procedures will not make for effective interviewing. Yet we do not conceive interviewing as a private and incommunicable art. It is not necessary that the interviewer improvise anew, out of whole cloth, in each interview. Experience suggests a more tenable point of view than either of these two.

We assume that there are recurrent situations and problems in the focused interview, many of which can be effectively handled by communicable and teachable procedures. From this standpoint, the "art of interviewing" consists of the following elements:

1. recognition of *typical situations and problems* with which the interviewer is confronted;
2. knowledge of probably effective and *previously developed* procedures for coping with each type of situation; and
3. *skill* in the application of these procedures.

A manual can do little for the last of these, which is a matter of capacity trained through experience. In interviewing as in other kinds of human activity, there are individual differences in the skill with which more or less standardized knowledge is put to work. But the proficiency of even the least capable can be considerably improved by bringing them to recognize certain types of situations which recur in the interview and by acquainting them with an array of flexible, but more or less established, procedures for dealing with these situations. A manual for interviewing is not a substitute for the exercise of individual skill and judgment; rather, it provides some tools with which skill and judgment can operate.

In this connection, an instructive parallel is provided by the art of diagnosis in medicine. It is commonly recognized that a skilled diagnostician does not necessarily have a more extensive or profound body of *formulated* knowledge than his less able colleague. Often he has developed, in an unformulated though not unformulable fashion, an array of insightful discriminations and generalizations which mark him off from the run of diagnosticians. Indeed, the subculture of medicine is such that physicians acquire great prestige and other social rewards from colleagues as a result of dramatic episodes of quick and valid diagnoses.[15] Despite such acknowledged individual differences in diagnostic capacity and skill, schools of medicine continue to provide training in diagnosis on the firmly grounded assumption that some measure of proficiency can be acquired from such instruction. As with the diagnostician, so with the inter-

---

15. See, for example, the observations of a noted diagnostician, David P. Barr, M.D., "The making of a diagnosis," *Boletin de la Asociacion Medica de Puerto Rico,* XLI (May, 1949) , 139-147. "Many of us have been impressed with the diagnostic acumen of some one of our teachers, usually a man of immense experience, who by a few well-directed questions and a brief inspection has rendered with an air of authority or perhaps with elaborate casualness an absolutely correct diagnosis. No one of us can escape a desire to emulate a performance so effective and dramatic. The danger of yielding to this desire cannot be exaggerated. The peril is increased if one of us in the near past has been lucky enough to attach a correct label and thus have gained some prestige among our colleagues. The reputation of a professional humorist is not harder to maintain than that of a great diagnostician. Snap diagnoses usually consist of little more than a perfunctory label, a recognition of one aspect of a problem which usually requires prolonged study for its true understanding. Undue emphasis upon one facet may impair a consideration of the whole."

viewer: the practices and precepts which have been developed through cumulative experience can serve as a basis for training. Thereafter, variations in individual capacity will distinguish the more from the less skillful practitioners of the art.

Plan of the Manual

Since it is simply one among several kinds, the focused interview of course involves all those considerations which are common to the use of the interview as a tool of social research. We shall not, however, be concerned with the problems and techniques of interviewing in general; these are amply treated in various handbooks and articles.[16] Such matters as the selection of interviewers, interviewer bias, the recording of data, the maintenance of rapport—these and other such standard aspects of the interview are largely neglected here in the knowledge that they are fully and suitably discussed elsewhere. We shall consider instead the strategy and tactics which are more or less distinctive of the focused interview.

As we have said, the procedures for eliciting significant data will be discussed, so far as possible, in connection with the four major criteria of the focused interview. However, since certain further problems at once arise when the focused interview is conducted with groups, rather than with a single person, we shall also devote a chapter to procedures which have been found useful in the group interview. There are

---

16. W. V. Bingham and B. V. Moore, *How to Interview* (New York: Harper, 1941) ; Pauline V. Young, *Interviewing in Social Work* (New York: McGraw-Hill, 1936) ; Eleanor E. and Nathan Maccoby, "The interview: A tool of social science," in Gardner Lindzey, (ed.), *Handbook of Social Psychology* (Cambridge: Addison-Wesley Publishing Company, 1954), I, pp. 448-487; Paul B. Sheatsley, "The art of interviewing and a guide to interviewer selection and training," in Marie Jahoda, Morton Deutsch and Stuart W. Cook (eds.), *Research Methods in Social Relations* (New York: Dryden Press, 1951), II, pp. 463-492; Herbert H. Hyman, *Interviewing in Social Research* (Chicago: University of Chicago Press, 1954).

certain other problems which do not bear upon any one criterion of the focused interview in particular—such as the problem of maintaining an appropriate atmosphere for the interview, of curbing the expression of the interviewer's sentiments, or of having the interviewee adopt an expressive rather than a "consultant" role. Matters of this kind will be examined in the final chapter.

Throughout the manual, it will be noted, there is considerable emphasis upon misplaced or ineffectual procedures of interviewing. This emphasis is based on the assumption that proficiency in interviewing can be gained by learning from such errors of interviewing practice—errors which, once described and classified, can the more often be readily avoided.

The problems and procedures described in the manual are funded in clinical experience, primarily in the field of social research on mass communications. The formulations derive, for the most part, from reflections on experience compounded of trial and error and from psychological and sociological theory. The comparative utility of the procedures has not been put to controlled experimental test. On the contrary, with the focused interview as with other types of interview, there is still much room for systematic research on the worth of alternative techniques.[17] But short of rigorous experimental inquiry, there is also room for efforts to codify and to assess techniques on a clinical basis. That is the character of this manual.

---

17. As represented, for example, by the considerable beginnings of research by Herbert Hyman and his associates dealing with sources of error in the interview; cf. Hyman, *op. cit.*

CHAPTER II

{ Retrospection

The Reporting
of Circumstantial Detail

The primary objective of the focused interview is to elicit as complete a report as possible of what was involved in the experience of a particular situation. Without detailed reports, the clinical data resulting from the interview will not encompass the qualities of range, depth, specificity and personal context essential to an understanding of the nature and meaning of the responses.

Full-bodied reporting is not, of course, a criterion unique to the focused interview. Both the detailed psychological questionnaire and other types of single-contact "depth interviewing" seek to elicit a maximum of detail. But the focused interview differs from the run of these other inquiries because it centers on a particular set of experiences and because the objective characteristics of the situation in which those experiences have occurred are known to the interviewer (in contrast to life-history interviews, for example). This focal quality facilitates detailed reporting in at least two ways:

1. Instead of having to make extensive explorations to identify relevant experiences, the interviewer can begin at once to explore the significant aspects of the particular experience.

2. Because the interviewer is familiar with the objective nature of the situation, he can provide cues which enable the interviewee to recall it more vividly.

This chapter, accordingly, examines cues to reinstatement of the original experience and the ways in which this facilitates the reporting of definitions of the situation in circumstantial detail. The retrospection which derives from such reinstatement is essential if the major criteria of the interview are to be satisfied.

Expediting Detail
through Retrospection

To capture all the details of an individual's definition of a situation would presumably require a complete and literal recording of his responses as they occur. The technique of the interior monologue—codified if not invented by the symbolist Edouard Dujardin and brought nearer to perfection by James Joyce—is one kind of literary device designed for the purpose of describing, in cinematic style, the imagined details of ongoing human experiences. In place of literary craft, we can conceive a technological contrivance— an introspectometer, so to say—which would record, in accurate and intimate detail, all that the individual perceives as he takes part in social interaction or is exposed to various situations. If the raw stuff of the experience is to be adequately recorded, this hypothetical machine would have to synchronize its record of the situation and the details of selective responses to it. It would provide, in other words, a motion picture of the individual's stream of experience as he is engaged in the situation. And to avoid the distortions that might result from intrusion of the apparatus into the situation, it would be necessary that the individual not be aware that the apparatus was at work.[1]

Since no such device exists at this writing,[2] the nearest equivalent available to the interviewer is to have each subject act as his own introspectometer during the interview. Were he to report wholly from unassisted memory, it is probable that his report would be thinned out at some points and elaborated at others after the fashion described by Bartlett[3] among others. To counteract such tendencies toward distortion and toward loss of germane data in the course of recall, it is helpful to *reinstate* the original situation under review.

Reinstatement for the purpose of detailed reporting involves two related processes on the part of the interviewee: recall of the *stimulus situation* to which he was exposed and recall of *his reactions* to it. Although this might most accurately be described as retrospective introspection, it is enough, perhaps, to refer to it simply as *retrospection*.

The difference between mere introspection and retrospec-

---

1. That such an instrument would make for a collective nightmare if it were used for anything but disinterested inquiry is evident, just as it is evident that it would be a powerful instrument for discovering new truths about human behavior.

2. Beginnings toward such an instrument have of course been made. The Lazarsfeld-Stanton program analyzer provides polygraphic recordings of positive or negative responses to an ongoing stimulus situation (a motion picture, radio program, etc.). Another approximation is found in experiments on perception which use the tachistoscope followed immediately by interviews with subjects concerning what they have seen. For a description of the analyzer and its operation, see Tore Hallonquist and E. A. Suchman, "Listening to the listener," in P. F. Lazarsfeld and F. N. Stanton, (eds.), *Radio Research, 1942-1943* (New York: Duell Sloan and Pearce, 1944), pp. 265-334; C. I. Hovland, A. A. Lumsdaine and F. D. Sheffield, *Experiments on Mass Communication* (Princeton: Princeton University Press, 1949), pp. 104 ff. For one among various summaries of the tachistoscope-and-interview procedure, see J. S. Bruner and L. Postman, "An approach to social perception," in Wayne Dennis, (ed.), *Current Trends in Social Psychology* (Pittsburgh: University of Pittsburgh Press, 1948), pp. 71-118.

3. F. C. Bartlett, *Remembering: A Study in Experimental and Social Psychology* (London: Cambridge University Press, 1932).

tion, as the term is used here, is essentially the difference between an individual's *present responses* to the situation and his recollection of *his responses at the time it was experienced.* This difference is illustrated in the words of an Army private taking part in a group interview on a movie they had seen:[4]

> *A.* Yes, and [they should show something] about colored WAACS.
>
> *Int.* When you are looking at a film the same as the one you just saw, do you find yourself wondering why there weren't any colored WAACS?
>
> *A.* Truthfully, I was really interested in the picture at that time and *I really didn't think of that,* but *now I do think of that.*
>
> In other words, the first response of *A* was on the basis of his present conception of the film, rather than a report of his reactions as he had watched it.

Retrospection in the focused interview, then, encourages stimulus-linked and detailed responses by helping the interviewee to *recall* his immediate reactions to the material rather than to *re-consider* the stimulus situation and report his *present* reactions to it.

Failures in Retrospection

Conversely, when retrospection is not encouraged by the interviewer, one or more of at least three types of reports have been found to occur, none of which gives an adequate account of the experience in question.

REPORTS UNLINKED TO STIMULUS SITUATION

When an interviewee has expressed a general opinion and

---

4. Many of the interviews quoted in this manual were with groups. In extracts from such interviews, the interviewer will hereafter be designated as *Int.* Interviewees *in each group* will be assigned identifying letters; when the same letters turn up in different quoted passages, therefore, they do **not** necessarily designate the same individual.

the interviewer follows up his remark with a question which does not instigate retrospection, the interviewee often elaborates his opinion without indicating whether the situation under review played any part in forming, maintaining or reinforcing his opinion:

A. I think this war could be won from a religious standpoint.

Int. In what way?

A. Well, I believe the German people, if they want their own views and hold up their own rights, they should . . .

The interviewer might have encouraged retrospection by referring to the stimulus situation in his follow-up question: "Was there anything in the film which gave you that impression?" Instead he asks an "introspective" question which invites elaboration of the expressed opinion. But the situation under review remains as obscure as before.

SUPERFICIAL REPORTS

When the interviewee is not encouraged to retrospect, much of the complexity and depth of his original response may be lost, either because he does not then recall his experience vividly or because he assumes the interviewer seeks his current opinion. In the following quotation, for example, *A* expresses his belief that compulsory military training is a good idea:

A. On the spur of the moment, you can't train a vast army . . . the younger they start [the better].

Since the interview is intended to assess an experience, not to tap a general opinion, it would presumably be in point to learn whether the film gave the interviewee this idea, whether he had it before and the film reinforced it, or whether it is entirely unrelated to the film. But instead of trying to have the experience reinstated, the interviewer asks a question which neither refers to the film nor to the interviewee's original reactions to it.

Int. Then how do you think our men would stack up against Axis troops?

A. I think it will be a battle against numbers and equipment.

Thus deflected from his original point of view, *A* simply gives a casual answer to what seems to be a question designed to elicit an opinion unrelated to the film. Here again, retrospection might well have been facilitated by asking "Did anything in the film give you that impression?"

REACTION TO INTERVIEW SITUATION RATHER THAN TO INITIAL SITUATION

Furthermore, if the interviewee is not encouraged to retrospect as well as to introspect, he appears more likely to respond primarily to the interview situation than to recall his response to the situation under review. He may try to decide, for instance, what the interviewer would like to hear from him, what the interviewer might find impressive. If it is a group interview, he may respond primarily to anticipated reactions of others to his report rather than focus on a recollected experience. These responses, unrelated to the objectives of the interview, seem the less likely to occur the more attention is centered on the reinstatement of an earlier experience.

Procedures Aiding Retrospection

Here, as throughout our review of suggested procedures, it must be emphasized that we are still very far from that condition in which cut-and-dried rules can be given to cover appropriate procedures and the timing of their use. On occasion, the interviewee will report his reactions only and the interviewer will want to help him reinstate the stimulus situation in order to gain clues to the elements or patterns evoking the reactions. At other times, the interviewer will want to help the interviewee express the full complexity of his reactions to some part which the interviewee has described as having had particular significance for him. Each of these interview situations calls for distinctive procedures, we believe, and these in turn will vary according to the stage reached in the interview.

But for purposes of exposition, these procedures must be considered in a certain sequence, and examples must be used from selected contexts. The sequence is in no way meant to reflect either order of importance or order of appearance in the interview, and it will frequently be noted that a procedure suggested as particularly useful in one context is also useful in others.

THE PROGRAM ANALYZER

As we have briefly suggested, the Program Analyzer might best be described as a one-dimensional introspectometer. It is an apparatus which enables individuals to record limited dimensions of their reactions to an ongoing experience, by pressing "like" and "dislike" push buttons (or by not pressing any buttons, which signifies indifference). The push buttons are connected with a pen which moves along a roll of tape synchronized with the stimulus situation (*e.g.,* a film or a radio program), thus making a permanent record of favorable, unfavorable and neutral reactions.

For present purposes, the Analyzer can be regarded as a device through which the interviewer can *partially* reinstate both the stimulus situation and the response. There are several occasions where reference to a recorded response may encourage retrospection. As a means of opening the interview, for example, the interviewer can, by referring to the graph of recorded ongoing reactions, point out a part where interviewees had indicated a definite evaluation:

> *Int.* We have a record of the film and the parts you liked and disliked . . . you remember the part of the film called "I Was There"? Some of you liked it and some of you didn't . . .

By mentioning a part of the film which apparently evoked decided reactions, the interviewer partially reinstates the *stimulus.* By referring to their general like-dislike *reactions* to it, he partially reinstates the response. By thus suggesting both the original stimulus and the immediate response, the interviewer encourages interviewees to *retrospect* before they report.

Or the graph may be utilized later in the interview, in much the same way, as a means of effecting a transition from one part of the original situation to another:

> *Int.* Another part of the film that some of you liked and some of you did not like is the part about the nurses and the Battle of Bataan . . . Some of you did not like it at all, I wonder why . . .

The Analyzer technique for facilitating retrospection has two main advantages: the graph informs the interviewer which parts originally had significant meaning *for the interviewees,* thus obviating the necessity of his having to select arbitrarily a part which may or may not have carried its share of meaning. The technique enables him also to refer to the ongoing reactions as a cue to reinstatement of the original experience.

A device such as the Analyzer is often not available for group interviews and it has not yet been widely adopted for use in individual interviews. For the most part, therefore, it is necessary for the interviewer to resort to other procedures (which can, of course, also be used in conjunction with the Analyzer) ; one of these consists of graphic re-presentation, the other, with almost endless variation, of verbal cues.

GRAPHIC RE-PRESENTATION OF ORIGINAL SITUATION

Perhaps the most realistic way to reinstate the stimulus phase of the original experience is actually to re-present parts of it. How this is done depends upon the subject of the interview: if the initial situation was a motion picture, stills taken from the film will serve the purpose; if a radio program, "playbacks" from a recorded transcription (notched and marked to permit ready identification) can be used; and if printed material, excerpts can be used.

Re-presentation of this sort is useful whenever an interviewee alludes to a part of the presentation and the interviewer wants

(1) to help the interviewee to recall it in order to facilitate detailed reporting of his responses;
(2) to verify the reference to ensure that interviewer and interviewee are focusing on the same section or,
(3) in a group interview, when he wants to ensure a common frame of reference for all interviewees.

By thus seeing or hearing the original stimulus situation again, the interviewee is helped to recall his reactions to it. The reinstated stimulus, it seems, helps reinstate the experience, which can then be the more fully reported.

> [Interviewee, an enlisted man in the Army, says he doesn't like to see wounded soldiers in a film.]
> *Int.* Why not?
> *A.* I don't know. It is just a matter of emotions. My feelings don't press towards that side of films.
> *Int.* It rubs you the wrong way? It irritates you?
> *A.* No, it's just that I don't know how to express it. It's emotional.
> *Int.* Well, if you think back to the time you were watching, what were your feelings?
> *A.* I felt that it was a sort of gruesome part of the film.
> *Int. You mean this scene here {holding up still picture}?*
> *A.* Yes, something like that. The public might have a reaction to that if they were exposed to it. Although some of them realize the fact that under battle conditions men must lose their lives or be wounded. Some people would say "Look at that" and it would lower their morale.

Here the interviewee has made a statement calling for further elaboration; he objects to the scenes showing wounded soldiers. When asked merely to "explain" he seems to be blocked. The interviewer then tries to lead him back to his earlier feelings by hypothetical suggestions, but the interviewee is unable to develop his report further. The interviewer then tries verbal cues to reinstatement: "If you think back . . ." but still elicits only general affirmations. When the interviewer holds up a still from the film, however, the interviewee apparently recalls his feelings at the time, and is able to express them. That he apparently disguises his reactions under a cloak of "some people" is a matter for later discussion.

Reinstatement through graphic re-presentation is also a useful way of getting the interview started on the level of detailed retrospection:

> *Int.* There was one part there that several of you did not like . . . I would like to get the story on that . . . That's the one about the machine shop where it showed this man [holding up still] who had turned his garage into a machine shop . . .
>
> *A.* And he made a speech. That should be cut out.

Sight of the picture apparently brings back to mind a detail which he had disliked, and the interview then proceeds on the retrospective level.

For similar reasons, graphic reinstatement is useful in making transitions from one phase of the interview to another:

> *Int.* Another part of the film I would like to get your slant on is the first part, training for invasion. A good many of you liked that. For example, this part where they are climbing the rope ladders [holding up still] and going over barbed wire [holding up still] and crawling along in the muddy field under machine gun fire [holding up still]. Do you remember that? What was interesting about that?

It will be noticed that the two preceding examples in which stills were used to open an interview or to effect a transition involved use of the Program Analyzer. The interviewer did not arbitrarily select parts of the film for reinstatement. By referring to the analyzer graph, he knew which parts had some degree of significance for the interviewees. Had he made the selection arbitrarily, he would of course have been structuring the original situation in his own terms, possibly selecting a part that had actually held little or no significance for the interviewees, but to which they might subsequently have attached significance simply because he pointed them out.

For these reasons, we have adopted the practice of using graphic reinstatement only of those parts of the situation spontaneously mentioned by interviewees, or, when Analyzer data are available, of parts which are known to have elicited responses at the time they were first presented. That the aspects of the situation which hold considerable significance for the observer often hold very little significance for the interviewee is one of the best-attested results of our clinical experience.

VERBAL CUES

These few illustrations may be enough to suggest that even when such aids as the Analyzer graph, stills and playbacks are available, they are not sufficient in themselves as a means of inducing sustained retrospection. They must usually be accompanied by appropriate questions from the interviewer. When these aids are not available, the interviewer's questions alone must be relied upon to bring about retrospection.

Verbal cues to retrospection may refer to the stimulus situation, to the response, or to both. They may be directive questions which describe the process of retrospection, or they may merely allude to the situation or to the response in a question ostensibly introduced to encourage the interviewee to continue his account.

1. *Questions referring to the process of retrospection.* Frequently, an interviewer can best encourage retrospection by simply referring to the components of the total experience under review. By this is meant that he refers in a general way to both the stimulus situation and the response without structuring them and suggests that the interviewee "look back" or "think back" on them. This technique seems

particularly in point at the beginning of an interview, where it serves to focus the interviewee's attention on his earlier experience from the very outset and thus helps establish a pattern for the interview. However varied the details of phraseology, the essentials of such questions remain much the same:

> Thinking back over the program, what stood out in any way?
> What parts would you say stood out most in your mind, as you think back on the film?
> If you think back on the film you just saw, did any part of it stand out in your mind?

At least three common aspects of these questions should be noted:

1. The interviewer *refers* to the retrospective process: "thinking back," "when you think back," "if you think back."
2. *He refers to the stimulus situation:* "the program," "the film."
3. And finally in asking for the response, he uses *the past tense:* "what . . . *stood* out," "*did* any part stand out?"

At first glance, there may not seem to be much difference between opening an interview with a question which asks for his impressions of the situation—"Well, what impresses you about the film?"—and one which directs the interviewee to his experience and only then asks for his impressions— "Thinking back over the film, what impressed you most?" In actual interviews, however, these seem to set off two quite different trends of report. The first question abruptly calls for a report, here and now, and often the interviewee mentions the first thing that comes to mind, which may or may not have impressed him at the time of the original experience. The second question, with its suggestions that he pause to "think back over the film," helps him to retrospect and focuses his attention on the earlier experience rather than on his current state of mind.

For substantially the same reason, a similar phrasing of questions has been adopted in effecting transitions from one area of interest to another. For example:

> *Thinking back over that experience,* what else stood out in any way?
> What other parts would you say stood out *as you think back* over the film?

2. *Questions including reference to the stimulus situation.* A further way in which to encourage and maintain retrospection is that of including direct and indirect references to the original experience in as many questions as possible. Elementary though it is, this procedure seems generally effective. The interviewer's allusions tend to curb the ever-present tendency to report current appraisals of past experiences by focusing the interviewee's attention on his original experience. There is, of course, the risk of becoming monotonously repetitive, and we scarcely assume that a monotonous and dull interview will be an instructive interview. But the risk does not appear unduly great, for there are numerous ways of referring to the original situation.[5]

3. *Verbal cues to past response.* When an interviewee refers to part of the stimulus situation, but does not indicate his reactions to it, the interviewer will want to facilitate retrospection in order to elicit a detailed report of the response. In this instance, his verbal cues to retrospection will aim to focus the interviewee's attention on his reactions to the situation rather than on a description of the situation itself.

> *Int.* How about the first part of the film?
> *A.* The one where they showed the little tiny boy?
> *B.* They were all assembled, the troops, and there were three men walking up. I didn't exactly see their faces, but drums were playing.

---

5. These are examined at length in Chapter IV.

Int. What did you think about when you saw that scene?
C. I thought they all looked like mechanical men.

Interviewees recall the details of the reinstated scene, but do not indicate their reactions to it in any way. Thereupon the interviewer explicitly directs their attention to their reactions at the time, and begins to elicit reports of response.

Here again, the use of the past tense has been found useful: the reference is not to the present reactions of interviewees—"What do you think about the scene?"—but to his past experience—"What *did* you think about *when* you saw that scene?" Of course, only systematic experiment could definitely establish this, but it is our repeated impression that continued use of the past tense by the interviewer helps appreciably to return the interviewee to his initial experience of the situation and to facilitate recall of his response at the time, whereas use of the present tense tends to elicit current opinions which may not be connected with that situation. Consider this synoptic case in point.

A. England was fighting to save her own neck.
Int. That is interesting. What *gives* you that impression?
A. Why, she is fighting to save her own neck. That is what everybody is fighting for.

Reference to the interviewee's reactions, then, is effective in facilitating retrospection primarily in those instances where the stimulus situation has been clearly reinstated. And when this practice is adopted, the seemingly trivial device of using the past tense is effective enough to be recommended as an integral part of the technique.

PITFALLS IN VERBAL CUES TO RETROSPECTION

1. *Structuring the situation or response.* In referring either to the stimulus situation or to the response, the interviewer may unwittingly impose his own structuring of the situation on the interviewee. This, we believe, should be avoided so far as possible. It is inexpedient to begin by *select-*

ing parts or aspects of the situation for discussion, thus *suggesting* a significant stimulus. Instead, the interviewer should use such general questions as "What parts stood out?" "What, in the film, impressed you in that way?" "What were your feelings?" *etc.* He should not prejudge the matter by *characterizing* the situation in a particular way:

> *Int.* What sort of impression did you get when you saw those scenes of thousands and thousands of Nazis massed in one group?
> *A.* Like a bunch of cattle with no brains.

The interviewer has designated a scene for discussion, but in making the reference he has colored it by the use of characterizing phrases such as "thousands and thousands" and "massed." The interviewer will consequently not know whether the interviewee's report was suggested by the characterization of the episode or by the interviewee's own impression of it.

He might have found some more general way of referring to the scene, as he did in the following instance:

> *Int.* I have been asking you about some of these scenes showing action in the film. Are there any others that stand out in your mind?
> *A.* That film where they had the freighters . . . how the people underestimated it. They never figured anything about that ship. It seems funny that the ship would pull into the dock that nobody would know what is going on . . .

In this case, the interviewee is evidently reporting something *he* thinks important, not reacting to the interviewer's description of it.

Similarly, the interviewer must avoid suggesting a *response:*

> *Int.* Well, when you were looking at this Nazi equipment, did you find yourself comparing it with ours?

In this instance, the interviewee's reply was "I didn't," indicating the irrelevance for him of the interviewer's suggested comparison. The interviewer was apparently thinking of his "interview guide" and trying to elicit information on a point that, in the content analysis, seemed to be significant.

The danger of introducing such suggested reactions is the same as the dangers frequently met in the questionnaire: the interviewee may feel forced to make the comparison, even though it had not occurred to him while he was watching the film. Had the interviewer used a directive question such as "What did you find yourself thinking while you were looking at the equipment of the Nazis?," he would have been more likely to elicit a report of the interviewee's actual reaction.

2. *Emphasizing sheer recall.* Faced with the necessity of reinstating some part of the stimulus situation, the interviewer may at once introduce questions such as "Do you remember the first part?," "Do you remember anything that stood out in the film?," or "What do you remember about that part?," in the hope of eliciting a report of the interviewee's reaction to the specified section. Frequently, however, this procedure merely helps reinstate the stimulus situation, without leading to retrospection.

> *Int. Do you happen to remember* these shots of the Belgian fort being taken by the Nazis?
> *A.* Yes.
> *Int. What do you remember about it?*
> *B.* They built a fort . . .
> *C.* They had maps . . .

The interviewer is apparently reinstating a scene with the intent of determining what was significant about it. But *A* interpreted his "Do you remember" literally and reports that he does remember. The interviewer then asks what is remembered, and elicits a report of remembered details.

Had he rather assumed that the interviewees remember the scene and asked an unstructured question about it, "You remember those shots of the Belgian fort being taken by the Nazis . . . What were your feelings about that?" he would have been more likely to elicit a pertinent response, in which reference to particular aspects of the scenes (maps, forts) would be on the basis of significance rather than of requested recall.

Again, in another case:

> *Int.* Well, one of you a minute ago mentioned the Nazi equipment in this film. *Do you remember* any of the fighting equipment?
>
> *A.* Yes.
>
> *Int.* What scenes do you think of especially?
>
> *A.* Their mechanized units.
>
> *B.* The way they moved the large guns from the other side of the country. He has two fronts there, I believe, and they moved them from one front to the other.
>
> *Int.* How was he able to do that so fast?
>
> *B.* He had all those highways built in advance.
>
> *Int.* *What did that make you think when you learned something like that?*
>
> *B.* Well, it seemed to me that the people in England and France and all those smaller countries must have been pretty much asleep to let all that go on in front of their faces. That is just a personal opinion.

Here the direct "Do you remember" question elicited only an affirmative reply. The interviewer must go on to ask what scenes the interviewee had thought of, and then to ask further for his reactions ("What did that make you think . . ."). Had he avoided the "Do you remember" part altogether, and first asked "What scenes brought out something about the Nazis' equipment one of you mentioned a minute ago?" he would have avoided the "memory" responses which shed little light on the interviewee's reactions to the film.

There are, of course, some instances where a "do you remember" question may immediately set off retrospection:

> *Int.* Do you remember the part where Churchill was talking?
>
> *A.* Well, Churchill was making a speech; that was at the declaration of the war. I don't remember the speech, but I have an idea, I remember what part of it meant, that in spite of the odds that they were going to carry

on for the sake of righteousness and it was their only choice.

But even here, the reactions have not been vividly reinstated, so the interviewer must go on and ask:

Int. How do you feel about hearing speeches by leaders of that kind . . .

The assumption that the interviewee remembers the scene leads to an emphasis on reinstatement of the total experience (both the stimulus situation and the reaction to it) rather than on *recalling* the stimulus situation. The resulting reports are therefore likely to be both more relevant and more detailed.

In such instances, retrospection can usually be better facilitated by *assuming* that the interviewee remembers the particular situation, and going on to a phrase which asks for his reaction to it:

Int. Do you remember the last part of the film . . . Can you remember what you thought of that part while watching it?

A. Men that lived for their country and nothing else.

B. . . . Them soldiers, they went out there to get France back again from the Germans.

Finally, it may be noted that repeated allusions to memory lead some interviewees to define the interview situation as essentially a *test* of memory. This is scarcely conducive to the informal atmosphere which is a prerequisite to an effective interview.

Summary

In short, retrospection is required to capture the subject's experience of the stimulus situation in circumstantial detail. Without such retrospection, interviewees may on occasion report reactions which are not linked to the stimulus, or which are superficial, or which are essentially reactions to the interview situation rather than to the original experience of the stimulus. There are various ways in which the interviewer can facilitate retrospection. If a Program Analyzer was used, he can refer to the tape, singling out those sections which elicited particularly favorable or unfavorable reactions. Or he can reinstate the stimulus by re-presenting parts of it—showing still shots from a film if a motion picture was seen, playing back sections from a recorded transcription, if a radio program was heard, and so on. In addition to such devices, the interviewer can facilitate retrospection through the kinds of questions which he asks. He can aid the interviewees by referring, in his questions, to the process of retrospection, by including references to the stimulus situation, and by making it clear that he is interested in past response.

CHAPTER III

{ Range

The first criterion of an effective focused interview to be considered in detail is that of *range:* the extent of relevant data provided by the interview. Without implying any strict measure of range, we consider it adequate if the interview yields substantial data which (1) exemplify types of responses to the situation which were *anticipated* on the basis of a prior analysis of the situation; (2) suggest types of *inter-relations* between responses to the situation which were obtained in some other way (for example, through questionnaires or observation); (3) bear upon aspects of the situation, and responses to these aspects, which were *not anticipated* on the basis of prior analysis. The greater the coverage of these three types of data, the more nearly the criterion of range is satisfied.

Gauging Range

In the nature of the case, there is no great difficulty in assessing the extent to which the first type of data (reports which indicate that anticipated responses do or do not occur) is being obtained in the interview. During the interview, the interviewer continually checks the reported responses against the interview guide (which, it will be remembered, involves hypotheses based on a prior analysis of the situation): to what extent has the interview dealt with the items set forth in the guide? As the interview proceeds, the interviewer will typically find that certain items in the guide have not been covered, and, consequently, that data bearing upon particular hypotheses have yet to be elicited. He can then move the interview toward these neglected areas. The capacity for this kind of successive checkup in the course of the interview can be greatly developed through experience; eventually the interviewer will find that he habitually engages in this sustained matching of interview and guide without having to make any special effort. In this way, the interview guide provides a crude measure of the adequacy of coverage so far as anticipated responses are concerned.

It is quite a different matter in the case of both the other types of data to be provided by the interview: data suggesting interrelations (cross-tabulations) between responses to the situation, and wholly unanticipated responses. In these instances, the rule is, in effect, the more the better. Put more formally, the interviewer should attempt to maximize the number of reports of unanticipated responses since this will make the interview a more fruitful source of new hypotheses. But it is patently not possible to say, even roughly, when the interview has elicited an "adequate" range of unanticipated responses, since one has no way of telling how many of these unanticipated responses to the situation did, in fact, occur. Yet, as we shall see, the maxim that the interviewer should search out as many unanticipated responses as possible is something more than a pious expression of hope. If the interviewer recognizes in advance the extreme importance of obtaining such data, he will be more likely to pursue vigorously those leads which seem to indicate that such an unanticipated response has occurred. Perhaps most important of all, the studied effort to elicit as much as possible of this kind of material may counteract the common tendency of interviewers to choke off interviewees' comments which do not fit closely into the interview guide. This emphasis on unanticipated responses thus helps the interviewer achieve that flexibility of the interview which serves to keep the free flow of expression going.

For these conjoint reasons, and within the practical limitations of a particular interview (the amount of time available for the interview, the number and variety of items on which interview data are needed, the depth and detail of material required about each of these items), *the interviewer should maximize the range of the interview by eliciting as many anticipated and unanticipated responses as possible.*

Fallacies in Seeking Range

We have noted that the focused interview presupposes an analysis of the situation under review and an interview guide largely based on this analysis. The interview guide contains a list of those aspects of the situation which, it is supposed, elicit significant types of responses. For each of these aspects, a tentative series of questions is included in the guide, questions which it is believed will elicit the type of interview data showing whether or not these (or other) responses have in fact occurred. But even when the interviewer recognizes that this is only a guide, he is often likely to use it as a fixed questionnaire comprising predesignated questions. As a result, one of the chief merits of the interview—flexible adaptation to emerging new data—is surrendered. Such misuse of the interview guide takes various forms. We shall consider, at this point, only those errors of use which interfere with obtaining a sufficient range in the interview.

FALLACY OF ARRESTING THE REPORTS

In the first place, there is an enduring temptation for the interviewer to confine himself to those areas of inquiry which have been set forth in the guide and to choke off comments which do not directly bear upon these areas. Interviewees' comments which do not fall within these pre-established areas of interest are often interpreted as "irrelevant." Of course, if they turn out to be truly irrelevant, if they do veer off in a direction which has no conceivable bearing on the matters under review, these digressions should and could be curbed (by the use of procedures to be described later). But often the interviewer, equipped with an interview guide, too hastily concludes that comments are irrelevant solely on the ground that they refer to aspects of the situation which were not included in the guide. There develops then the considerable danger of succumbing to premature and spurious judgments of irrelevance and thus arresting what is at times the most useful type of interview material: the unanticipated response.

> *Int.* Well, now what about the first part of the film? You remember they had photographs of the German leaders and quotations from their speeches . . .
>
> *A.* I remember Goering, he looked like a big pig. That is what that brought out to me, the fact that if he could control the land, he could control the people.
>
> *B.* He is quite an egotist in the picture.
>
> *Int.* Did you get any impression about the German people from that?

Here the interviewer introduces a section of the film for discussion. Before he finishes his remarks, one interviewee volunteers his impression and another begins his interpretation. Both remarks indicate that the interviewees seem to "have something on their minds." Being more attentive to his interview guide than to the implications of these remarks, the interviewer ignores the hints which might have added further to the range of the interview. He then asks the question, from his guide, which he had probably intended to ask in the first place.

FALLACY OF FORCING TOPICS

The interview guide may be misused to curb the range of the interview in another, though related, fashion: the interviewer may adhere too closely to the guide by *forcing* upon interviewees questions and topics which appear in the guide, but which do not tap or are not relevant to their actual experience. Whereas the fallacy of arresting comment consists in *cutting off prospective leads*, this fallacy consists in *imposing preconceived and irrelevant topics* upon interviewees. In both cases, interviewees have a sense that they are being coerced. Typically, they respond by suppressing part of what they have to say and the range of the interview suffers.

"Forcing" occurs when the interviewer intrudes a question before he has evidence that the interviewee has, in fact, been concerned with the matter to which the question refers. Often, the interviewer indulges in such forcing tactics only because he believes that he *must* introduce the topic or question which appears in his interview guide. The following case illustrates at some length the way in which forcing may occur and the blockage which it may entail.

> The interview dealt with a documentary film on the early conquests by the Nazis. The interviewer evidently wished to discover the conceptions of Nazi strategy which had been derived from the film, particularly in comparison with the strategy of the Allies. The interview guide had anticipated the possibility that the film might inadvertently lead to a devaluation of Allied strategy through contrast with the apparently superb strategy of the enemy. The interviewer introduces a direct question bearing on this:

> *Int.* How do you suppose—now that you think back on the picture—how do you suppose the Nazi strategy compares with the strategy of the Allied leaders?

> Quite apart from its other inadequacies, this "forced" question evidently interferes with the flow of the interview. There was no prior evidence in the interview that any in the group of interviewees had considered Nazi strategy in such comparative terms. The question did not directly correspond to their outlook, as may be seen from the sequence of comments on this question by the interviewees.

> *A.* Are you including all the world in that now?
> *Int.* Yes.

B. At the present or at that time?
Int. Well, at that time, first.

These queries directed to the interviewer suggest that the interviewees had not previously considered the matter of Nazi strategy in such comparative terms. In all probability, the questions represent an effort of the interviewees to gain their bearings in this unexpected context. The "problem" has been forced upon them; it has not been derived from their previous remarks. The irrelevance of the comparison suggested by the question breaks the continuity and flow of self-exploration of attitudes by interviewees as they begin, in effect, to ask the interviewer to "define his terms." The initiative of the interview passes into the hands of the interviewees: they do the questioning.

Additional indication that this particular comparison involved the forcing of comment is found in the further development of the interview. The interviewer evidently perceives that his question has led to confused and fruitless "answers." He fails, however, to diagnose the problem correctly and does not consider that this aimless talk may be largely attributed to the "irrelevant" and "unrealistic" comparison which he has *forced* upon the interviewees. In an effort to redirect their attention to the issue which so far is relevant to his interview guide, but not to their experience, he starts anew to establish *a common universe of discourse* by narrowing the terms of the comparison.

Int. Well, now, you remember the film, don't you, showing how the Nazis marched into France? [General assent]

Having fixed the attention of the group on this one component of the comparison, the interviewer repeats the forcing fallacy: he introduces essentially the same comparison which initially led to blockage and confusion and disrupted the flow of the interview.

Int. How would you compare the planning they showed there with our planning in North Africa? Which do you think was better?

The array of "answers" to this query indicates how ill-advised such a persistent forced comparison can be. Once again, another interviewee indicates by his counter-question that the comparison does not represent a mode of perception or evaluation which corresponds to his actual experience while seeing the film or thereafter. There is continued resistance against considering the comparison.

C. You say our planning in Africa? I haven't seen any.

Int. What do you mean?

C. They show the diagrams on the screen how the Germans went into France or captured Poland or Norway, but as far as Africa, I mean fighting towards . . . away from . . . Tunisia, I don't know.

D. I don't think you can compare them because they are all in different positions, not in the same countries.

In short, *forcing a topic upon interviewees continues to evoke resistance and does not advance the interview.* Instead of obtaining coverage of a topic contained in the interview guide, this procedure leads to a situation in which the interviewer is pitted *against* the interviewee. At long last, the interviewer comes to recognize the source of the impasse. He finally introduces a question which might well have been the one to initiate the discussion.

Int. At the time you were looking at the picture, did you get any idea of Nazi strategy in operation?

This question, if it does nothing more, at least elicits a direct response and evaluation of enemy strategy. It avoids the fallacy of forcing comment on a topic which has not previously been found relevant to the experience of interviewees; a fallacy which, in this instance, arose from the interviewer's insistence on following a line of questioning that had been set forth in the interview guide.

FALLACY OF ADHERING TO FIXED QUESTIONS

The foregoing case illustrates one way in which *excessively close adherence to an area of inquiry previously laid down in an interview guide may interfere with extending the range of an interview and,* for that matter, *with the development of the interview in general.* A related shortcoming occurs when the interviewer cleaves too closely to the wording of *questions* set up in the interview guide, rather than pursuing the implications of an interviewee's remarks. Although it is convenient for the interviewer not to have to improvise all questions in the course of the interview, the intended asset of pre-established questions may easily become a liability.

When the interviewer recognizes that interviewees are alluding to an area of inquiry previously defined in the guide, he is likely to introduce one of the standardized questions contained in the guide. This is all well and good *if* the question happens to be appropriate in the particular case. But unproductive interviews are those cluttered with the corpses of fixed questions which proved to be irrelevant. For often, the interviewer, imbued with certain fixed questions dealing with a particular topic, *does not listen closely and analytically to the interviewee's comments and thus fails to respond to the cues and implications of these comments, substituting, instead, one of the routine questions from the guide. If the interviewer is primarily oriented toward the guide, he may thus readily overlook the unanticipated implications of the interviewee's remarks.* In this way, the interview guide may be converted into a rigid set of shackles, interfering with the *flexibility* which is one of the assets of the interview. This is essentially misuse, rather than use, of the interview guide. It misconstrues the function of the guide, which is designed primarily to provide an array of relevant areas for inquiry to be covered in the interview. It is essentially a checklist to ensure adequate coverage of items relevant to predefined hypotheses; it is not intended to serve as a fixed and rigid schedule which will preclude reports of unanticipated responses to the situation under review.

The following short excerpt from an interview illustrates the way in which the interviewer may abruptly introduce a question from his interview guide which proves to be largely irrelevant to the implications of the interviewee's previous comment.

  A.   I say those pictures were the most interesting pictures because they were real. I have seen them in New York and Newark newsreels.

Several implications of the remark might have been drawn by the interviewer as provisional hypotheses: (1) belief in the authenticity of a documentary film increases interest in the film; (2) some but not all parts of the film are possibly regarded as authentic; (3) familiarity with scenes and sequences, previously seen in other institutionally legitimized films such as newsreels, may possibly lead members of an audience to conclude that the entire documentary film in which these sequences occur is authentic. But instead of directing his further questions toward developing some of these possible implications, the interviewer *raises a new issue* by introducing a question from his interview guide.

Int. How do you think we got those pictures of Hitler, for instance?

This invites the reply:

A. From all over. Russian pictures . . . I have seen them pictures when Hitler invaded Poland taken by Polish aviators.

This leaves still unanswered and unelaborated the specific questions raised by the interviewee's initial comment. Instead of possibly obtaining a fresh set of reports dealing with the general problem of what leads documentary films to be regarded as authentic or as spurious, the interviewer resorts to a fixed and, within this context, an irrelevant question derived from his interview guide. Another and extreme case in point further illustrates how misplaced adherence to queries derived from the guide involves the introduction of issues which are irrelevant to interviewees.

Int. Did anybody feel that he had always believed the British to be good tough citizens and, therefore, the picture did not teach them anything new or give them any information?

A. I haven't even given it a thought.

The foregoing examples clearly indicate that *predetermined questions should be used only when they correspond to the implications of interviewees' prior comments or when they tentatively initiate a fresh topic for discussion.* They should *not* be used as followup questions merely because they deal in some sense with the general topic. Such routinized uses of fixed questions serve to retard rather than to advance the objective of obtaining a wide range of comments in the interview.

FALLACY OF RAPID SHIFTS

In striving to obtain as wide a range as possible, the interviewer may be too easily satisfied with cursory discussions of many different topics. In reaching out for range, he may sacrifice depth. To be sure, within the limits of time available for an interview, it is not always possible to cover many areas of inquiry in a thorough fashion. But there is small point in nominally covering an extended series of topics, if the interview data on each of these are negligible. The very purpose of the interview is vitiated if topics are considered so briefly that the interviewer learns only that the situation in question has elicited some kind of attitudinal response (e.g., that this part of a radio program was "liked" and that part "disliked"). In short, *the canon of extending the range should not be confused with a canon of superficiality.* The following case illustrates the sterility of comments elicited by a series of questions which shift rapidly from one topic to another:

> *Int.* Well, now, the next part of the film is about nurses coming back from Bataan and Corregidor. Most of you seemed to like the raids on Manila. Tell me a little about that.
>
> *A.* I didn't care for that . . . I have seen those films before. I have seen them so many times they are not interesting to me. They are the same pictures as in the newsreels.
>
> *B.* I enjoyed it. Maybe we will be under the same attack.
>
> *C.* I didn't care for it.
>
> *Int.* Why not?
>
> *C.* We all know all war is hell more or less. You see one bombing raid and you have seen it all . . . it is not interesting.

Int. What about the next section? Surrender of Americans at Bataan? Most of you seemed to find that interesting. What did you find interesting in that?

D. I don't know. It didn't make me feel good to see Americans surrendering to Japs. Maybe we will be able to take back that dishonor some day. It is not dishonor to surrender. They fought like hell.

Int. Do you like to see films of that sort whenever it is possible to show them?

E. I do. I like action films very much, rather than other kinds. I like to see what happened when they finally do take a place . . . You see what they did with prisoners and things. I like to know those things. Anything with action and battles I particularly like, because especially when they started to bomb and the people got panicky, more or less see what is the wrong thing to do. By seeing what happened to them by getting panicky, you won't get panicky.

Int. Remember the story told by the Army nurse? What did you think of her story . . . ?

F. I didn't pay much attention to it at all. I just watched the picture.

Int. I have to rush this, much as I would like to talk at greater length. Let me ask one or two questions about the WAACS. Some of you found it interesting, and some of you didn't . . .

B. I don't like it. Not interesting at all to me to see what a woman is doing. I imagine they make good mechanics . . .

In this instance the Program Analyzer was used, so the interviewer knows what scenes had impressed the audience of interviewees in one way or another. The purpose of his questioning, therefore, is to determine *what it was about* each scene that led to these Analyzer responses of like or dislike, what evaluations meant in terms of the attitudes, expectations and perceptions of the interviewees.

The interviewer reinstates a scene with his first question, and this leads to two responses, both of which need to be followed up if their meaning is to be learned. What does it mean that *A* loses interest because he has seen scenes of this kind before? Why did the impression that "we may be under the same attack" make it "enjoyable" for *B*? Instead of following up these thin and preliminary reports, the interviewer pauses only for a few further remarks by *C* without exploring further the implication that this soldier prefers not to see scenes of bombing raids.

Instead, the interviewer shifts to another section of his interview guide. This begins to elicit a set of affective connotations from one interviewee, but in place of developing these or of eliciting their responses from others of the group, the interviewer proceeds with yet another question of the kind which virtually casts the interviewee in the role of a "consultant" on the making of films. In this case, *E* replies with a specific report of his reactions—a more useful report than this kind of question ordinarily elicits. Yet here again, instead of finding out the reactions of the rest of the group, the interviewer goes on to introduce still another topic. He receives only one response, largely empty of meaning. This time, he becomes aware that he is flitting quickly from one question to another, acknowledges his fault—"I have to rush this"—and compounds his error by hurriedly turning to still other matters. "Coverage" has become an uncriticized end in itself. The mere hasty allusion to the remaining questions in the guide is taken to discharge his obligation as an interviewer—he becomes oriented toward his own behavior as an asker of questions rather than maintaining the role of an unhurried and interested listener. This extreme case of substituting the mere appearance of coverage for the central purpose of obtaining pertinent data clearly exemplifies the danger of seeking to maximize range at all costs.

It is dubious whether the interviewer should devote *any* attention to topics which are not explored beyond the points reached in the foregoing example. The quick "once-over" technique wastes time. It diverts interviewees from their own foci of attention, without any compensating increases in the interviewer's knowledge about selected areas of inquiry. In view of the shortcomings of inducing rapid shifts in discussion, we suggest the working rule: *Do not introduce a particular topic unless a sustained effort is made to explore it in some detail.* The principal "exception" to this rule is the case where an interviewee introduces a patently promising lead in the course of discussing another topic. A transition to the new topic is then justified, providing the interviewer takes note to revert to the incompletely discussed topic later in the interview.

Procedures

We have repeatedly said that there are few hard and fast rules for the focused interview. This is all the more in point when we consider procedures intended to satisfy selected criteria of an effective interview. The following discussion serves only to illustrate some types of procedures which appear to extend the range of interviews; they suggest rather than prescribe.

For the most part, the tactics considered in this manual have been found useful at every stage of the interview. But the procedures primarily designed to extend range do depend, in some measure, on the changing horizons of the interview: on the amount of coverage already obtained, on the extent to which interviewees spontaneously continue to bring in new subjects, and on the amount of time still available. The interviewer must therefore be vigilant in detecting transitions from one stage of the interview to another, if he is to decide upon the procedures most appropriate for widening range at each stage. Above all, he will utilize these procedures when interviewees prove to be relatively inarticulate.

UNSTRUCTURED QUESTIONS

The unstructured question as a tool of the focused interview is considered in several sections of the manual. Repeated reference to this type of question is to be expected precisely because it serves several purposes of the interview simultaneously. It leads to specificity of comment, it invites spontaneity, it can be readily adapted to elicit depth reports and, most pertinent to this chapter, it is a means of obtaining a wide range of comments.

As we have noted, use of the unstructured question is particularly appropriate in the early stages of the interview. This will afford a preliminary range of items to be followed up later. But in every stage, unstructured questions of the following kind can be used intermittently to extend the range of comments beyond that anticipated in the interview guide:

What else in the situation caught your attention?

This type of unstructured question is especially pertinent whenever a particular topic has been adequately covered in the interview and interviewees' comments do not provide an easy transition to another area of inquiry. This procedure may not at first come easily to the interviewer. When he notes that the interview lags as a topic is virtually exhausted, he may be tempted to resort to direct questions such as:

What did you think about the part where . . . ?

In general, however, the degree of the interviewer's direction should be minimized and opportunities for interviewees to indicate areas of significance should be maximized by avoiding this practice and by introducing nondirective questions instead.

As the interview develops, this type of question no longer elicits fresh materials. It is a sign that a new phase has been reached in the interview, so far as range or coverage is concerned. Interviewees then require added assistance in reporting foci of attention. From this point, the interviewer introduces new topics either through transitions suggested by the interviewee's remarks or, in the final stages, initiates topics drawn from the interview guide which have not yet been explored. The first of these procedures utilizes *transitional questions;* the second, *mutational questions.*

TRANSITIONAL QUESTIONS

Typically, the interviewee and the interviewer will both make occasional transitions from one area of discussion to another, but whether these are interviewee-controlled or interviewer-controlled, continued consideration of the objectives of the interview will help the interviewer decide when they are in order and how they are to be utilized.

1. *Interviewee transitions.* One of the more general precepts drawn from our experience holds that, within wide limits, *it is preferable that the interviewee, rather than the interviewer, make the transitions to new areas of discussion.* But this can become an uninstructive and, at times, misleading maxim unless one recognizes the limits within which it is taken to apply. The interviewer who possesses what H. A. Murray has called "double hearing" will soon infer from the context of such spontaneous shifts of subject that they have various functions for the interviewee and that each kind of transition calls for distinctive tactics by the interviewer.

Of the several reasons for shifts engineered by the interviewee, four will be considered here:

1. The topic under discussion is peripheral to the interviewee's own interests and feelings, so that he seeks to escape from this irrelevant subject.
2. He seeks to escape from an area of discussion for a diametrically opposed reason: it is imbued with deep affective significance for him, and he is not yet prepared to verbalize his feelings.
3. He shifts to a new area which is of central significance to him, abandoning the one which is of somewhat less concern.
4. He has talked at length about a particular subject and, having exhausted what he has to say, he moves the interview onto new ground.

When the interviewer has reason to suppose that the shift is symptomatic of Types 1 or 4, there is little use in taking note to revert to the area of discussion which has just been abandoned by the interviewee. Transitions of Type 1 signify that it would not be fruitful to attempt any further exploration of an area which is simply not pertinent to the experience and feelings of the interviewee; transitions of Type 4 signify that the interviewee sees no *further* relevance in a given area, although the interviewer may later seek additional discussion of the area if he detects certain aspects, pertinent to his hypotheses, which have not yet been considered. In general, however, transitions 1 and 4 may be regarded as signposts that the topic can be safely abandoned and that it will probably not arise spontaneously later in the interview.

If, however, the transition is of the second kind, this signifies that the timing of the discussion is premature and that postponement is indicated. In this type of case, it is clearly advisable to have the interview revert to the sensitive zone at a later time, preferably by drawing upon an appropriate spontaneous remark by the interviewee. A more direct reversion can be safely adopted with regard to the third type of transition: since the abandoned topic is of some significance to the interviewee but has simply been overshadowed by a topic of more central significance, it is feasible to turn back to the temporarily by-passed topic, particularly when the interview guide suggests that it bears upon certain hypotheses.

All this assumes, of course, that the interviewer can infer, with some degree of assurance, which of these types is represented in the interviewee's change of subject. The sheer identification of the four types is of some help, reminding us that transitions are psychologically not all of a piece. Furthermore, by attending to the behavioral contexts of a transition, the interviewer can often gain clues to its psychological meaning. In Type 1, the interviewee commonly manifests no affect in talking about the initial topic, but merely lack of interest. He has little to say about it from the beginning, exhibits signs of boredom, lets his attention drift and, altogether, shows that the topic is, for him, simply dull.

The interviewer can usually recognize transitions of Type 2—escape from an emotionally sensitive subject—by the character of the interviewee's responses to the topic he seeks to avoid. He has difficulty in expressing himself, or refuses to do so; he seems to resent or vigorously objects to "depth" or "personal context" questions about the topic. In these cases, it can be provisionally assumed that he is escaping from a painful or highly emotionalized subject by introducing an alternative one. Insistent concentration on this subject serves little purpose. Reticences are not necessarily fixed, however, and as rapport is strengthened, a once-taboo subject can be re-introduced as the interviewer "proves" by his behavior that he does not pass judgment but is capable of both detachment and interest.

When the interviewee has contributed little by way of response to a particular subject, but evidences no blockage or little emotional involvement with it, his transitional statement is probably of Type 3, moving to a new area which holds more significance for him. The interviewer can often recognize this kind of transition by the more enthusiastic or interested tone and manner of the interviewee as he introduces the new topic. Here again, except for the case of a group interview where other interviewees manifestly have something more to say on the abandoned topic, there is little occasion for the interviewer to revert to it.

The fourth type is usually the least difficult to detect: the interviewer's questions about a subject begin to yield diminishing returns, until finally it is clear that the interviewee has little or nothing left to say on the topic. When he introduces a new subject in this instance, there will of course be no reason for reverting to it.

2. *Interviewer transitions.* Generally preferable though it is to have transitions effected by the interviewee, there

are, nevertheless, occasions when the interviewer will have
to bring about a change of topic. When the criteria of range,
depth, specificity and personal context have been satisfied for
the topic, when the interviewee does not spontaneously introduce another one, and when unstructured questions no
longer prove effective, it is obvious that the interviewer must
introduce a transitional question if he is to tap the reservoir
of response further. The other occasions on which he is well
advised to make a transition is when the discussion has gone
far afield, or has become generally tedious. In the former
case, to insure adequate coverage, and to avoid the reporting
of much irrelevant data, it is advisable to introduce a stimu-
lus-related topic. In the latter case, the topic should be shifted
at the first signs of boredom or antagonism, since, if such
attitudes are allowed to persist in connection with one topic
they may continue, to its detriment, throughout the interview.

It is usually possible for the interviewer to adopt either of
two types of transitional questions. He can make use of association of ideas to introduce a *cued* transition or, as the interview progresses and he accumulates a series of items which
require further discussion, he can effect a *reversional* transition.

In a *cued* transition, the interviewer so adapts a remark
or an allusion by an interviewee as to ease him into consideration of a new topic. This has the advantage of maintaining the flow of the interview rather than abruptly turning
the attention of the interviewee to something entirely new.
In each of the following short examples, the interviewer
gradually shifts the discussion to a new subject by drawing
upon an interviewee's phrase or remark:

> *Int.* Well, now you mentioned combat troops a moment
> ago. Did you get any impression as to how well the
> Nazi troops are trained, or how poorly trained they
> are? What about that?

> *A.* I think the side that has the most equipment and who know how to operate these things successfully will win the war.
>
> *Int.* Well, did you get any idea from the film of the way in which the Nazis operate?
>
> ――――――――――
>
> *C.* In Poland . . . the Nazis . . . directed their military operations against the civilians as well as the army. . . .
>
> *Int.* Now what about these operations against civilians? . . . What did you think of when you saw those scenes, let's say, of the destruction of Warsaw for example?

Cued transitions may require the interviewer to exercise considerable ingenuity. In the following case, avowedly cited as an extreme, even bizarre, example, the interviewee was wandering far afield from the subject under discussion, but the interviewer picks up a cue and refocuses the interview:

> *A.* The finest ingenuity in Germany that you ever saw. They are smart. But I think this: I don't think when this World War is over that we won't have another war. We will. We have had them since Cain killed Abel. As long as there are two human beings on this earth, there's going to be a war.
>
> *Int.* *Talking about Cain,* he could be called something of a small-time gangster, couldn't he? Do you happen to remember anything about gangsters being brought out at any point in this program?
>
> *A.* Dillinger. That was where . . .

Although the interviewer's association is more than a little far-fetched, it served its purpose. Had the interviewer simply changed the subject—"What did you think about the gangsters in the program?"—he would have indicated that he thought the interviewee's remarks irrelevant, with a consequent strain on rapport. As it was, the cued transition led to ready discussion of the new topic.

When the time for an interview cannot be greatly extended, the cued transition enables the curbing of patent digression, without prejudice to rapport.

Reversional transitions are those effected by the inter-

viewer in order to obtain further discussion of a topic previously abandoned, either because the interviewee had avoided
it or, in a group interview, because someone had moved on
to a new theme.

Wherever possible, the reversional question is cued, i.e.,
related to the topic currently under discussion. It can, for
instance, take this form:

> That suggests something you mentioned previously about
> the case in which . . . What were your feelings at that point?

When it does not seem possible to relate the reversional
query to the current context, a "cold" reversion may be
productive.

> *Int.* A little while ago, you were talking about the scenes of
> bombed-out school houses, and you seemed to have
> more ideas on that. How did you feel when you saw
> that?
>
> *A.* I noticed a little girl lying under a culvert—it made me
> ready to go fight then. Because I have a daughter of my
> own, and I knew how I would feel if anything like that
> happened to her. . . .

This kind of reversional query is seldom used, however,
and only in instances where it seems likely that the interviewee has "warmed" up to the interviewing situation sufficiently to be articulate about the topic he had avoided
earlier.

In order to insure adequate coverage, it is useful to introduce cued or reversional types of transition questions whenever unstructured questions are no longer productive and
the interviewee does not effect a transition himself.

MUTATIONAL QUESTIONS

Toward the close of the interview, there may still remain
important points to be covered. Failing opportunity for a
cued transition, the interviewer may have to introduce a

mutational question, which contains an explicit reference to a previously unconsidered area.

> How did you feel about that part of the talk which dealt with the use of drugs in an X-ray examination?

Ideally, there should be little occasion for mutational questions. The more skillfully the interviewer uses unstructured questions, the more alert he is to cues afforded by interviewees, the more carefully he notes items to which he should revert, the less need for mutational questions. At best, they should be considered a last resort—not because any one mutational question can disrupt the interview, but because, on the whole, the focused interview seeks to provide an easygoing and open occasion for the interviewee to express *his* sentiments and perceptions of a situation. As soon as the interviewer introduces a mutational question, he structures the situation for the interviewee to some extent, and may tend to force him into a discussion which is remote from the interviewee's own perception of the situation:

> *Int.* Oh, yes . . . a point in the film none of you has mentioned. I would like to find out something about it. You remember the shot in the film of Dillinger?

Here the interviewer has introduced a scene without structuring it appreciably, characterizing it only by a reference to Dillinger.

> *A.* Yes, the gangster. The end had come to a man that thought he could get away with everything.

A is the only one in the group who responds, however, suggesting that the scene may have had no central significance for other interviewees. This inference is further confirmed by the fact that again only *A* responds to the follow-up question:

> *Int.* What did that bring out?
> *A.* That brings out that one man can have too much power and get by with it all the time until a certain time.

This illustrates the chief reason for avoiding the mutational question whenever possible. The interviewer's question attaches significance to a topic which it apparently did not have for the interviewees themselves. It therefore elicits neither range of evocative elements and patterns in the stimulus situation nor range of response.

Mutational questions should be kept at a minimum for an additional reason. When introducing a new topic in this way, the interviewer seems more than usually apt to ask *a series* of questions in rapid succession, in order to obtain a response to a subject which he supposes may not have much significance for the interviewees, since they did not bring it up themselves.

> *Int.* There are two or three other parts of the film I would like to talk about for a minute. Nobody has mentioned the part showing the strategy of the Germans in France. Remember the map showing just how they operated and then the explanation by an intelligence officer? Do any of the rest of you remember that part of the film? Did you find yourself pretty well bored by that kind of discussion or do you feel you have learned something from it? If you had your choice, would you want that to be in the film or cut out?

The interviewer in this case would plainly have been well advised to stop after referring to "the part showing the strategy of the Germans in France." Instead, he virtually adopts the role of a schoolmaster informing pupils that they had "overlooked" a matter of seeming importance ("Nobody has mentioned . . ."). Then, responding to his own awareness that this "oversight" might mean that the scenes had not registered at all, he proceeds to identify them. Not content with this degree of structuring the stimulus situation, he goes on to make suggestions as to how the interviewees might have responded to these scenes ("Did you find yourself pretty well bored or do you feel you have learned something?"). Still reacting to this sense of urgency, he finally defines their role as that of a consultant and asks for their judgment of the value of retaining these scenes in the film. In short, the interviewer structures the stimulus situation, converts the interview into a seeming check on the adequacy of the audience's perceptions, suggests a probable response and converts the interviewees into consultants. All this evidently stems from his gratuitous assumption that mutational questions must be many and varied, if they are to provide a foundation for the change of subject. The compounding of questions by the interviewer is a frequent sign, as we shall see, that he is in a part of the interview which he finds stressful and difficult to control. It is characteristically expressive rather than instrumental behavior on the part of the interviewer. But a rapid and unbroken sequence of questions seldom accomplishes the end in view.

Under other circumstances, a mutational question may elicit a good range of response, particularly when the new subject turns out to have had central significance for the interviewees:

Int. You remember those pictures of the Nazi leaders in the film? Where do you suppose they came from?
A. Espionage.
B. Captured film.
C. I believe that showed right there we had a secret service organization working in those countries at the time. I believe that. I don't believe the German people would have allowed us in there with cameras and such as that if they knew they were bringing them back here. I believe if they had taken pictures like that they wouldn't be in a position where we could get hold of them, so naturally I believe we have some agents in there. . . .
D. They were made in this country and faked, that is the impression I got . . . [and so on].

The interviewer has asked a mutational question, which is relatively unstructured. As the discussion proceeds, it becomes apparent that this component of the original situation had aroused many-sided responses in the interviewees.

In this instance, the question of the authenticity of the films had been spontaneously raised in a previous interview, so the interviewer felt that he was on fairly safe ground in introducing it. This illustrates another basis for the choice of mutational questions designed to extend coverage of the points included in the interview guide: those subjects which proved to have been significant in previous interviews can be introduced, with some assurance, as new subjects in later interviews. This somewhat reduces the likelihood that the new subjects will be wholly irrelevant to interviewees.

In general then, mutational questions should be used as a last resort. When there is no alternative, they should be as general and unspecific as possible.

To summarize, the criterion of range suggests that the interview should yield as many anticipated and unanticipated responses as is possible within a limited time. There are a number of fallacies to be avoided in the process of extending the range of the interview. One of these is the fallacy of arresting comment, of cutting off promising leads before they have been fully developed. Another is the fallacy of imposing preconceived and irrelevant topics upon interviewees without evidence that the interviewees have, in fact, been concerned with the topic to which the interviewer refers. Third, there is the fallacy of adhering to fixed questions, which makes it unlikely that the interviewer will be oriented toward the discovery and exploration of unanticipated responses. There are procedures for avoiding these fallacies and, at the same time, extending the range of the interview. The most general of these, particularly appropriate at the opening stages of the interview, is the use of unstructured questions. As the interview proceeds, however, these unstructured questions may no longer elicit fresh leads. Then other types of questions become more appropriate. For example, when a topic has been fully explored and unstructured questions no longer produce fresh material, then transitions to a new topic may be effected either by the interviewer or by an interviewee. And toward the close of the interview, if important points still remain to be explored, then the interviewer may have to introduce a mutational question, which contains an explicit reference to a previously unconsidered area.

CHAPTER IV } Specificity

Research Functions of Specificity

A major objective of the focused interview is that of lessening and ideally of closing the gap between interviewees' *perceptions* of a situation and their *reports* of what they have perceived. We assume that specific and detailed accounts of how the situation was defined supplement clinical and experimental observations of overt behavior by affording clues to the salient parts, patterns and attributes of the concrete situation which evoked that behavior. Thus, specificity is, at one and the same time, a criterion of any effective focused interview and, as discussed in Chapter I, a prime objective of some interviews.

In the study of real-life situations rather than, say, in nonsense-syllable experiments on rote memory, there is all the greater need for discovering the meaning attributed by subjects to elements, aspects, or patterns of the complex situation to which they have been exposed. Thus, in one such study, army trainees reported that "the scene of marching Nazi soldiers" in a documentary film led them to feel anxious about their ability to withstand the German army. This report does not satisfy the canon of specificity. Anxiety may have been provoked by the impression of matchless power symbolized by massed armies; by the "brutal expressions" on their faces to which the commentary referred; by the elaborate equipment of the enemy; by the extensive training seemingly implied by their maneuvers. Without further specification, there is no basis for selecting among the several possible interpretations.

In stressing the need for specificity, we do not at all imply that people respond to each and every element of the total situation as a separate and isolated item. The situation may be experienced "as a whole" or as a complex of configurations. Individual patterns may be perceived as figures against a background. But we cannot rest with such facile formulations; we have yet to detect the "significant wholes" to which response has occurred, and it is toward the detection of these that the criterion of specificity directs the interviewer's attention. It is only in this way that we are led to findings which can be generalized and which provide a basis for predicting selective responses.[1] Inquiry has shown that, as a significant whole, brief scenes in a motion picture, for example, have evoked different responses, quite apart from the fact that seeing-a-film-in-conjunction-with-two-thousand-others was *also* a "configurative experience." But without inquiring into specific meanings of significant details, we

---

1. An overcondensed case illustrates this point. Following a series of tests of documentary films, the hypothesis was advanced that audiences retain items of information presented in the form of "startling facts" of the type exploited by the Ripley "Believe-It-or-Not" column. Such items have attention value; they stand out as a figure against the ground. They have diffusion value, readily becoming part of the currency of small talk ("Did you know that . . . ?") . And they have confidence value: they are "cold facts," as idiom so aptly puts it. On the basis of such tentative formulations, it was hypothesized that a "startling fact"—namely, that the first American casualty in this war occurred as early as 1940—would be one of the most notable informational effects of a documentary film. This proved to be the case, with a differential of 36 per cent between the experimental and the control groups. Without focused interviews, the differential effects of different phases of such a complex situation as a forty-minute film would be difficult to anticipate. It should be emphasized, however, that these are no more than they purport to be, namely, *hypotheses,* and that it still remains for these to be checked experimentally. For cases in point, see Hovland, Lumsdaine and Sheffield, *Experiments on Mass Communication,* pp. 92-94.

surrender all possibility of determining the effective stimuli patterns. Thus our emphasis on "specificity" does not express allegiance to an "atomistic," as contrasted with a "configurational," approach; it serves only to orient the interviewer toward searching out the significant configurations. The fact of selective response is well attested; we must determine what is differentially selected and generalize these data.

In studying the "effects" of particular situations—for example, changes in racial attitudes affected by residence in an interracial community or the attitudinal effects of a motion picture—it is common practice to refer the change to the total situation, or to *gross segments* of the situation. The canon of specificity directs attention toward the search for determinate elements or patterns in the situation which were involved in the changed responses. Whether the study is oriented toward theory or practice, it is advanced by in-creasingly specific knowledge of the effective elements of the situation.

As a first example of differences in the degree to which a significant part of a total situation has been specified, consider these remarks by two enlisted men explaining their interest in part of a film describing the process of training troops for the invasion of Europe:[2]

    A. It was something new.
    B. *That part going over the fence was interesting.* Going over the fence on those rifles, that was new. We never had anything of that kind.

Both men have expressed their interest in the same part of the film, and both have said that they liked it because it was "new." But the scanty remark by *A* provides no basis for telling *what* was new: the general character of this intensive training, the tactics used in invasion, or some particular

---

2. For a detailed account of the film evaluation from which the following extracts are drawn, see Hovland, Lumsdaine and Sheffield, *op. cit.*, pp. 108-117.

aspect of this kind of training; the response by *B* begins to indicate just what it was about the sequence of scenes that most impressed him.

Another example:

> *Int.* We'd like to get the story on that; particularly when the Secretary of the Navy came to give him the 'E' flag. You remember that?
>
> *A.* I don't like speeches and things like that. I like to see action pictures or something like that.
>
> *B.* I feel the same way; I don't care much for speeches.
>
> *C.* I think we had a majority of speeches since we are in the Army. We don't like to hear speeches.
>
> *Int. Anything about this particular kind of speech* that rubbed you the wrong way?
>
> *D.* Why such honor to a four-man machine shop? That is one reason. Four men couldn't run a machine shop to such advantage. I don't believe. . . . If it was a big shop, they would get the same credit and employ 3 or 5,000 men, probably 10,000.

The quest for specificity leads the interviewer to follow up the general expressions of "attitudes toward speeches" with the question: *"Anything about this particular speech that rubbed you the wrong way?"* The idiomatic phrase "anything *about*," refers interviewees to the specific *aspects* of the scene to which they have responded and elicits replies which suggest that it is not "a speech" as such, or the form of the speech which antagonized the enlisted men but the "exaggerated" kudos extended to what was, after all, a relatively insignificant unit in American war industry. There is an intimation here, which can now be further explored, that the interviewee responded to this symbolic scene from an instrumental perspective. Clues of this kind are provided by helping interviewees to specify the salient attributes of perceived components of the situation.

In other words, the more concretely interviewees are led to designate what was significant for them, the more germane the resulting data for a theory of attitude change: the more specific the account of perception, the more information it provides about the putative meanings of the elements, aspects and structures of various kinds of situations. And similarly, the more exactly the person reports just *what* he was responding to, the more the data serve the applied purpose of suggesting appropriate changes in the "product."

Processes of Specification

The preceding pages may have clarified the differences between merely identifying the gross *parts* of a situation which have evoked a particular response and leading interviewees to specify in detail the significant *aspects* of those parts.

Specification in the focused interview, however, not only requires the interviewee to designate significant aspects of the stimulus situation, but also to *link* particular responses to these. At times, the interviewee becomes quite explicit about some aspect of the situation as he has perceived it without going on to describe in comparable detail what it meant to him (his *response*). This provides data about his powers of perception and of recall, but is less than adequate in providing data about patterns of response to variously defined situations. The objective is to achieve substantial symmetry of report: a particular response should be linked to the aspects of the situation evoking it just as perceived and remembered aspects of the situation should be assigned meaning by being linked to the response.[3]

Not infrequently, interviewees will spontaneously specify both the evocative aspects of the situation and the character

---

3. This might be called *specification of response,* by analogy with the *specification of the evocative situation.* To specify a response, however, is to meet the criteria of "depth," "scope" and "personal context," each of which is considered at length in this manual.

Since the various procedures for obtaining detailed reports of response are considered later in the manual, we shall restrict use of the word "specification" or "specificity" to the stimulus situation. This will not, however, preclude discussion of a two-way linking process: the linking of responses to the evocative situation as described above, and linking of the specified aspects of the situation to the responses they evoked.

of their response, as can be seen in the two short examples that follow:

> *Int.* What about the next section [showing the] surrender of Americans at Bataan? . . . What did you find interesting in that?
>
> *A.* . . . it didn't make me feel good to see Americans surrendering to Japs. . . .

> *Int.* What brought that out, for example [that the Germans were ruthless]?
>
> *B.* The evacuation of the people in smaller towns and scattering them out in the roads to blockade the advancing troops. That isn't any warfare I would want to put over if I were at the head of it.

In the first excerpt, *A*, asked for his response, alludes to his feelings and goes on to indicate what it was about the scene that distressed him. He includes a specification of the stimulus in beginning to report his reactions. In the next excerpt, *B* exhibits the complementary pattern: asked to specify the stimulus situation leading to the inference that the Germans were ruthless, he specifies it, but goes on to elaborate his response.

With the desiderata of both kinds of specificity in mind, the interviewer is alerted, at each phase of the interview, to the need for eliciting more data of one or the other kind.

Procedures

Turning now to the matter of procedure, we consider the appropriate time at which to ask questions designed to have the interviewee specify the evocative aspects of the situation. Although this is not a matter of cut-and-dried rules, one procedure in particular seems more productive than others.

SPECIFICATION OF SITUATION AFTER RESPONSE

Two sequences of report predominate in a focused interview. When a particular part of the situation has been pointed out (either by the interviewee or by the interviewer) the interviewee seems to recall either his *reaction* to the reinstated part of the situation or some *aspect* of the reinstated part which impressed him. The first of these sequences generally seems to elicit more specific reports, for at least two reasons.

(1) Once the salient part of a particular situation has been reinstated and the interviewee reports the aspects of that part which impressed him before he reports his *response* to it, there is a considerable possibility that the *remembered* and *reported* aspects are not those which evoked the response:

Int. . . . There was a drawing of a castle which represented France and then the castle started to crumble. Do any of you remember that?

A. Where the emblem was crawling up?

B. Nazi termites.

Int. What was that intended to bring out?

C. Fifth columnists, propaganda.

In this case, the scene is specified before the response and the interviewer then asks: "What was that intended to bring out?" Two further elements of the scene are specified but there is little evidence to indicate whether these were merely remembered or whether they were indeed the basis for inferring that espionage and propaganda were at work. This procedure characteristically makes for dissociation of perceived-and-remembered items and of response.

(2) There is a further advantage in asking for responses before asking for further specification of the stimulus situation. Reports of response are likely to include some account of the evocative situation. By asking for a response first (once the stimulus situation has been reinstated), the interviewer encourages the interviewee to link his response with its source at the outset, rather than imposing an artificial dichotomy of stimulus and response upon him.

Experience suggests the following as an effective sequence of procedures designed to help interviewees specify the evocative aspects of the situation:

1. Reinstatement of a part of the stimulus situation and

eliciting general indication of what proved most significant to the interviewee.

2. Report of interviewee's responses to this part.
3. Specification of aspects of the designated part which evoked the response.

This is approximated in the following example:

Reinstatement of stimulus situation	*Int.* How did you feel when you saw that? . . . [bombing of Warsaw]
Initial report of response	*A.* I felt like jumping in.
	B. I did too.
	Int. What was it about that section that made you feel like that?
Specification of pertinent aspects of situation	*B.* . . . Wars are supposed to be fought with the military, *not going around bombing innocent women and children.*

When the interviewer assumes the initiative, as he primarily does only in opening the interview or in making transitions, he can usually arrange for this preferred sequence by phrasing his question in such a way as to call for the response first:

You seemed to like that part . . . *what were your feelings about that?*

Think back to the time you were watching that section. *What did you think of it?*

Any other *reactions* to that part of the film?

In contrast are the kinds of questions which call for specification first:

What didn't you like about that?

What do you remember most about that scene?

What did you find interesting in that?

Judging from experience with the focused interview, then, specification of salient aspects of the situation should be elicited after the general response to a gross part of the situation has been reported. Further procedures for eliciting specificity in this sequence and in other, less effective but possibly more frequent, sequences will be considered later in this chapter.

EXPLICIT REFERENCES TO STIMULUS SITUATION

The value of having the interviewer's question refer to the stimulus situation has been indicated in the chapter dealing with retrospection, where it was shown that such references tend to reinstate the original experience, thus helping the interviewee to report his perceptions and responses in greater detail. The occasions on which these references are appropriately directive or nondirective, explicit or implicit has also been reviewed in that chapter. At this point, we consider procedures which most effectively make for specificity of reporting. The following instance exemplifies the kind of specificity encouraged by *explicitly asking* that the report of response be linked to the stimulus situation.

[The interviewee has indicated that "you can't trust the Nazis."]

Int. What in the film brought out this idea that you can't trust the Nazis?

A. In every phase of it. When they made their promise that after Czechoslovakia there would be no more, and especially after they had Austria.

Here the interviewer's specific reference to the film has apparently helped the interviewee reinstate the stimulus situation with sufficient vividness to point out two aspects of it which elicited his expression of attitude.

Questions such as these refer explicitly to the document or situation which is at the focus of the interview. When the reference to the stimulus situation is only *implied* by the interviewer, as in the case that follows, the ensuing report tends to turn to generalities rather than to specification:

> [Interviewee observes that if the Allies had combined they could have stopped Germany.]
>
> *Int.* When Hitler was building up his army, did any nation want to stop them? How about that? Do you remember anything about that?
>
> *A.* Czechoslovakia wanted to stop them.

Had the interviewer asked "What did the film show about that?" the stimulus situation would probably have been sufficiently reinstated to enable the interviewee to report the aspect of the indicated scenes which had led to his inference.

We have found that unless the interviewer refers to "scenes in this film," "parts of this radio program" or "parts of this situation," interviewees are likely to shift toward the expression of generalized attitudes or opinion. Indispensable as such ancillary data may be, they do not take the place of reports in which responses are linked to the evocative situation. Yet it is only with difficulty that the inexperienced interviewer is weaned from his embarrassment over the seeming monotony of repeated references to the stimulus situation. Preferring variety of phrase to productiveness of interview, he becomes elliptical and resorts to implicit allusions. The ease with which this leads interviewees to shift to generalized opinions is brought out in the following excerpt:

> *A.* The German people were armed but they covered it up.
> *Int.* You think we didn't know about it?
> *A.* Yes.
> *Int.* Who do you think was asleep at the switch? Why didn't we know?
> *B.* I imagine their country was so well policed. . . .

Here the interviewer is obviously trying to discover what it was in the film that led the interviewee to believe that the Germans were secretly armed. His follow-up questions are so general, however, that not only does he *not* get a film-linked specification, but the interviewee turns to mere conjecture, just as another interviewee does in the following extract:

Int. What were we doing at that time, according to the film? Do you remember anything in the film that brought that out?

C. We were building up our own country after the war, trying to get our men at work.

Int. What about France and England, what were they doing all the time Hitler was rearming?

D. I *imagine* they were very much asleep and they were also living up to the Versailles treaty. I *imagine* they did not put faith in them. . . .

In his first question the interviewer refers to the film and the interviewee is reasonably specific about the reason for Americans' lack of attention to rearming in Germany. It might be supposed that, once the stimulus situation had been reinstated, the interviewer would not have to refer to the film in his next question, but as the subsequent remarks indicate, the interviewee is not specifying anything in the film which leads to his conclusion. This illustrates, in brief, the utility of *continuing to refer to the stimulus situation in specifying questions.*

It should not be concluded, however, that mere reference to the stimulus situation is enough to *ensure stimulus-linked specificity.* Situations of the following kind are not uncommon:

Int. Was there anything in this film that brought out the idea [that German children were being taught that Germany was mistreated during the last war]? . . .

A. There was a film I think I saw during my first week in the army. . . .

Here the interviewer has referred directly to the film, but the interviewee's reply is definitely not linked to it. In such a case, he repeats his reference to the film, "Yes,—was there anything *in this film* . . . ?"

Again, one encounters interview situations in which questions alluding directly to the stimulus situation nevertheless evoke only generalities.

[Interviewee has commented on the strength of the German army.]

Int. What impression did you get of the strength of the German army from the film?

A. They are well trained.

Int. Better trained than American soldiers?

B. Overtrained.

C. They are well trained all right.

D. Not any better trained, no.

Although the interviewer refers to the stimulus situation at the outset, there is no specificity in the reply. The next question might then have been "Was there anything in the film which gave you that impression?" Instead, his further questions, unlinked to the film, elicited only generalities.

Much clinical experience of this kind rather uniformly suggests that when the interviewer seeks to elicit specificity he should explicitly call for progressive specification.

In summary, then, specificity can be most definitely elicited by the use of nondirective questions: the most effective and least obtrusive point at which to elicit specificity is after a response to a particular part of the situation has been reported, and it is most *likely* to be forthcoming if the interviewer's question contains a direct reference to the stimulus situation. An obvious, but essential, observation must be added to this brief summary of general procedures which facilitate specificity: *accounts of response should not be discontinued until it is reasonably certain that the interviewee has designated every aspect of the stimulus situation which was relevant to the response.* In short, because of its great importance for the purposes of the focused interview, the interviewer should persist in his efforts to elicit specificity.

Selected Problems in Facilitating Specificity of Report

It has been pointed out that the most effective procedure for having the evocative situation specified is to start by reinstating a part of the stimulus situation; second, to help the interviewee designate the significant elements in that part; third, to ascertain his response to it; and finally, to determine the particular aspects of these selected elements to which he responded. It was also said, however, that this preferred sequence does not always, or even usually, obtain, and that there are several other kinds of occasions turning up in the focused interview which call for specifying questions by the interviewer. The major objective of this section is to identify various types of interview situations in which "specifying" questions are required and to suggest procedures for coping with these situations.

INTERVIEWEE INDICATES RESPONSES TO PART OF STIMULUS SITUATION

Consider, first, the "preferred" sequence. A segment of the stimulus situation has been reinstated, either spontaneously by the interviewee ("I like the part where . . . .") or by the interviewer (with verbal cues or graphic re-presentation). The interviewee has reported his general response to it. The next step is for the interviewer to interpolate "specifying" questions, which in this case serve two functions: they locate the significant aspects of the designated segment, and they encourage further and more elaborate reports of response. The following excerpt from an interview illustrates the first of these functions:

> *Int.* What about that part?
> *A.* Showed you what you are up against. Real facts. Showed you what you have to go up against when you are fighting.
> *Int. What do you think brought that out?*
> *A.* Lots of things, suffering, brutality of Japs and bombing of Manila gave you an idea of what is going to happen.

This shows how a specifying question locates the significant aspects of the scenes in a film which an interviewee singled out for attention as showing "what you are up against." For him, what's past is prologue: the behavior of the Japanese is indicative of their character just as the first episodes of the war are indicative of things still to come.

There is little variation in the type of specifying question available to the interviewer in instances of this kind. As exemplified above, it should be unstructured ("What about that . . . ?"), and it should contain a specifying reference to the stimulus situation ("What, in the film, gave you that impression?"). This general pattern can be varied somewhat by adapting to the interviewee's initial response, but the variations are slight:

> *A.* I didn't like it at all.
> *Int.* What rubbed you the wrong way? If you think back, what didn't you like about it?

> *A.* The idea was not to have a two-front war. He knew it was on his conscience to get rid of England and France, and they had to be put out then or there was no treaty because Russia was next in line.
> *Int.* What gives you that impression, that the Russians were next in line?

> *A.* That is, to compare Hitler's tactics with the gangster tactics and to show that they are practically the same.
> *Int.* In what way?
> *A.* They are moving into places and stealing and robbing and destroying.

Or sometimes the interviewer may encourage specificity by asking for it in so many words:

> *Int.* What gives you that impression . . . *What brought that out?*
> *A.* It showed it in the picture where. . . .
>   *or*
> *Int.* What brought that out *particularly?*

In short, eliciting specificity when the interviewee has begun to indicate his reaction to a gross stimulus situation simply requires one to ask for further details about the evocative aspects of that situation. The essential point is that this step in the focused interview should not be inadvertently neglected: specificity should be elicited whenever the stated response is linked only to the gross stimulus situation rather than to a characterized part of it.

PROGRESSIVE SPECIFICATION

When an interviewee has reported his response to a particular sector of the stimulus situation, the process of specification begins by having him first search out evocative aspects of the situation and ends by having him narrow down his perception of each of them. The process might be likened to a large searchlight which sweeps over the landscape, then, searching out significant landmarks, the lens is narrowed and the light focused on one point after another until every detail of any importance has been lighted up.

When a passage of a diary, a scene in a motion picture or a sequence in a radio program has been singled out as significant to an interviewee in a particular sense, his shifting perspective on that part is at first akin to that of the hypothetical searchlight: it sweeps over the entire part in question. With the help of the interviewer's questions, he then narrows his focus and picks out one or another aspect. But the matter need not rest there. What were the shadings, the nuances, of this particular perception? What other details were perceived? The interview continues to deal with the selected part and focuses on still another significant aspect until it illustrates the aspects which would be lost in a "full on" view.

The interviewer's question considered in the preceding section—"What in the situation gave you that impression?"— serves primarily to narrow the lens of the interviewee's attention:

A. They are very ruthless. . . .

Int. What brought that out, for example?

    A. Where they walked into a tunnel and started bombing
it.

Unless the interviewer continues his questioning, he will
not know what it is about this bombing of a tunnel that
made the Nazis seem ruthless. Why is it not taken simply
as an acceptable military tactic? And without further questions, the interviewer will not know whether there was anything else in the film which led the interviewee to conclude
that "they are very ruthless."[4]

Clinical data of the kind pertinent for understanding the
basis of the response begin to emerge with the allusion to
"where they walked into a tunnel and started bombing it."

The same sort of question found useful for eliciting initial
specification can also be utilized to obtain *further* specificity.
It is unstructured and refers to the stimulus situation. In
this type of instance, however, the reference to the situation
can be more specific since the interviewee has already singled
out the effective part of the situation (and the interviewer
therefore does not risk imposing *his* structuring of it upon
the interviewee).

    Int. Was there anything else in that part of the film that
        stood out in your minds?
    A. I watched the expressions on their faces [Americans
        surrendering at Bataan].
    Int. What kind of expressions?
    A. They took a beating, didn't feel good, but it was inter-
        esting.

Inasmuch as the interviewee has already selected "expressions on their faces" as significant for him, the interviewer
rightly picks up this allusion and goes on to seek characterization of these expressions that aroused his interest.
He might have said "Why" or "What about them" but by
definitely picking up the specific reference and repeating it,

---

4. The problem of finding what *else* in the situation elicited a particular
response involves the general problem of *range* and was discussed in the
chapter devoted to that criterion. Our present concern is with the problem
of *further* specification and characterization of a particular evocative stimulus.

the subject is encouraged to think back over his earlier perception.

Although the interviewee's initial singling out of the salient stimulus enables the interviewer to be more specific in the formulation of questions aimed at "further specification," it does not seem advisable for him to advance beyond the point of the interviewee's own specification.

A. They are well trained.
Int. What gives you that idea?
A. The way they march.
Int. You mean the goosestep?
A. The close order drill.

The interviewer makes his "further specifying" question too specific here. He jumps at conclusions and misinterprets the interviewee's *characterization* of the way the Germans march. The results are not misleading in this case, but some interviewees might well have thought "If he thinks the goosestep is the important thing, it must be" and as a result have answered in the affirmative regardless of their own perceptions.

This excerpt illustrates the utility of continuing to seek further specification. It is clear that something in the "way they march" has been taken as a sign that "they are well trained." The next question was apparently asked to discover which attributes of marching carried this significance. However, the interviewer advanced beyond the interviewee's own interpretation and began to impose his own interpretation of the significant symbol. As it happens, this interviewee was not suggestible; he rejects the interviewer's misplaced suggestion of "the goosestep" and, as infantrymen sometimes will, takes smoothly executed "close order drill" as a sign of thorough training.

When the interview is focused on responses to a document (film, print, radio program, *etc.*), further specification is helped by graphic re-presentation of the portion of the document which has been singled out for attention:

Int. Do you remember the section about the WAACS?

> *A.* I liked the part where they were doing KP. That is just what I think they should do.
>
> *Int.* This thing here [holding up still from the film]?
>
> *A.* That's it. At least the dishes will be washed by experienced hands. I've had too many dirty dishes. *That's just where they belong.*

There is no indication that the director of this documentary film had intended to activate attitudes toward appropriate sex roles in the armed forces. Nor had a prior content analysis included the hypothesis that this scene would carry this distinctive meaning for enlisted men. But the interviewer's sustained effort to uncover the symbolically significant attributes of this scene led to a new hypothesis which could be checked in other interviews. The canon of specificity is directed toward this function of instituting hypotheses which, as a matter of record, had not been formulated before preliminary interview data came to hand. Specificity commonly has heuristic value.

Re-presentation of a selected portion has turned out to be more effective than verbal requests in eliciting progressive specificity of reporting. Not only does the re-experiencing of the significant part of the document refresh the interviewee's memory of his original perception, but the mere physical fact of its being re-presented commonly leads him to elaborate his report.

Repeatedly, we see the necessity for establishing the symbolic meanings of the situation, if observed "effects" are to be adequately interpreted. Thus tests in 1943 showed that documentary films concerning the Nazis increased the proportion of men in experimental groups who believed that Germany had a stronger army than the United States. Inasmuch as there was no explicit indication of this theme in the films, the "effect" could have been interpreted only conjecturally, had it not been for focused interviews. Interviewees who expressed this opinion were prompted to indicate its source by questions of the following type:

> Was there anything in the film that gave you that impression?

It soon became evident that scenes which presumably stressed the "regimentation" of the Nazis—e.g., their military training from an early age—were unexpectedly taken as proof of their exceptionally thorough training, as the following excerpts from interviews indicate:

> It showed there that their men have more training. They start their men—when they are ready to go to school, they start their military training. By the time they get to our age, they are in there fighting, and they know as much as the man who has been in our service eight or nine years.
>
> By the looks of them where they took the boys when they were eight and started training them then; they had them marching with drums and everything and they trained them for military service when they were very young. They are well trained when they are grown men.

Thus the search for specificity yielded a clue to the significant scenes from which these implications were drawn. The interpretation of the experimental effect rests on the weight of cumulative evidence drawn from interviews and not on mere conjecture.

This case serves to bring out the need for progressive specification. If the subject's report includes only a *general* allusion to one or another part of the film, it is necessary to determine the particular *aspects* of these scenes to which he responded. Otherwise, we lose access to the often *unanticipated symbolisms* and private meanings ascribed to the stimulus situation. A subject who referred to the "regimentation of the Nazis" exemplified in "mass scenes" is prompted to indicate the particular items which led to this symbolism:

> *What about* those scenes gave you that impression?

It develops that "goose-step parades" and the *Sieg Heil!* chorus are taken as symbols of regimentation:

> When it showed them goose-stepping out there; it numbed their mind. It's such a strain on their mind and body to do that. Just like a bunch of slaves, dogs—do what they're told.

In general, then, "further specification" is in order whenever the interviewee has reported a significant reaction to a designated section of the stimulus situation. In substance, this involves use of some version of the stock question, "What was it in the [situation] that gave you that impression?" It can often be facilitated by including a reference to the interviewee's previously reported response. Where the means are available, graphic re-presentation can be used effectively to encourage further specificity.

CONNECTING RESPONSES UNLINKED TO SITUATION

As we have noted, the interviewee's report of his response is often *wholly unlinked* to the stimulus situation, or is vaguely related to the situation as a whole. Before the interviewer reaches the point where he can facilitate a report of the *aspects* which gave rise to the response, it is clear that he must have the response *connected* to pertinent parts of the situation.

A. It was so repetitious too.

Int. What kind of things did you notice were being repeated?

A. Well, the X-rays that had to be taken. He talked about the kidneys and the heart and so on. It wasn't necessary.

The interviewer tries to link the judgment of repetitiousness to the pertinent parts of a radio program under review. The first step meets with some measure of success, inasmuch as the interviewee does indicate the cases in point. This sets the stage for the next step, not taken in this instance, of ascertaining why these reiterated episodes led to a sense of superfluous repetition whereas other reiterated episodes in the same program did not.

It will be noticed that the phrasing of questions designed to link responses to evocative stimuli are often the same as those designed to have the interviewee specify further a part of the situation which has been linked with a response: "What brought that out?" or "What gave you that impression?" But in contrast to the questions aimed at "further specification," where the interviewer facilitates specificity by repeating the interviewee's characterization ("What kind of expression? What sort of points?"), the interviewer will find it useful to include reference to the interviewee's response or interpretation:

> *A.* . . . Russia was next in line.
>
> *Int.* What gives you that impression, that the Russians were next in line?

Or he may rephrase the subject's response slightly:

> *A.* There seemed to be a mystery about the X-ray pictures.
>
> *Int.* You mean that in explaining the term "X-ray" it wasn't fully explained?
>
> *B.* It certainly wasn't. I would be interested to know the difference between ordinary photographs and X-rays and he didn't explain that. . . .

Such reference to the response in the question serves to keep the interviewee from going off the track to specify a significant stimulus, but not the one evoking the reaction he has just reported. This kind of digression is most likely to occur in a group interview:

> *Int.* Do you think, judging from the film, that the Germans plan to invade the U.S.?
>
> *A.* No, it would be foolish. . . .
>
> *Int.* What in the film made you think that?
>
> *B.* Japan has more interest in the U.S. than Germany.

Had the interviewer asked "What in the film made you think that Germany will not invade the U.S.?" *B* would have been less likely to insert his unlinked comment, and *A* more likely to designate the bases for his inference.

GUIDING REFERENCE TO THE SITUATION

In the interview, as in other social situations, persons will periodically deliver themselves of general opinions and sentiments which have been activated by the give-and-take of conversation. The type of interview designed to search out deep-seated personality trends or values of long standing will of course encourage the expression of such sentiments. But in the focused interview, centered as it is on identifying the definitions of particular situations, it is essential to learn whether these sentiments were actually engaged in those situations. When the interviewee states a general opinion, therefore, the interviewer is plainly called upon to discover whether this is at all linked with the situation under review. As in the example that follows, a direct reference to the situation frequently helps the interviewee to be more specific, and makes it less likely that he will wander off on a path which, interesting though it may be in other connections, has little to do with the matter in hand.

> *A.* The German people were an aggressive nation throughout all history and there should be taken steps to punish them.
>
> *Int.* Do you remember any scenes in this film that gave you that impression?

Occasionally the interviewee will make a generalization, and go on to specify one part of the stimulus situation which led him to his conclusion. It remains for the interviewer to learn whether other elements or patterns in the situation evoked that conclusion. An effort of this kind is made in the following passage:

> *A.* The French were prepared to fight a defensive war; therefore the French depended wholly on the Maginot line. . . .
>
> *Int.* Was there anything *else* in the film that might have given you the impression that the French in this war were pretty much on the defensive? . . .

  B. The French waited . . . they sat and waited in corridors
and didn't try to go out. . . .

  C. . . . and a little bit of communism . . . moved in and
sort of softened up the people.

 Int. Was there anything in the film as you remember that
gave you the impression that the communists were
spreading pretty widely in France?

  C. Not in this film.

In this instance the interviewer follows up the remark
by *A* that the French lost because they were on the defensive and relied wholly on the Maginot line. He refers to the
film, and *B,* retrospecting, recalls another part that gave him
the impression that the French were on the defensive. This
apparently suggests another thought to *C,* but since he does
not link this up with the film, the interviewer asks a further
question which leads *C* to report that his impression did
not come from the film.

When the interviewee voices a general idea which he does
not relate specifically to the situation under review, the interviewer can often elicit such relations by appropriate kinds
of questions. The following examples may be enough to
bring out the character of questions which serve this purpose:

  That is an interesting point. *What about the film* from
that standpoint?

  Was there anything *in the film that brought that idea out?*

  You mentioned the precision of the German troops. Do
you happen to remember *anything of the film that brought
that out especially?*

  That is an interesting point. Do you happen to remember
anything *in the film* that might bear that out, that might
have given you that impression?

These repeated references to the film, particularly when they
are abstracted from the flow of the interview, may appear
abounding to excess. If they were left out altogether, it might
seem, the reference to the situation under review—the film,
in this example—would surely be there by implication. In-

deed, there are no ready-made precepts for deciding on the optimum frequency of explicit reference to the situation. As a matter of experience, these can be relatively few and far between when the interviewee is launched upon a detailed account of his responses to a situation (as we shall see later on, in our discussion of implied allusions). But when he is engaged in a series of general expressions of sentiment or belief or opinion, then there is occasion for explicit and repeated references to the situation, if the interview is not to move off on a tangent:

A. It's propaganda.
Int. Did anything strike you as being propaganda along those lines?
A. That's all you get *in the papers.*
B. You see it in any of the places, in the movies or papers. In nine times out of ten, you see things not as it actually happens.
Int. Did anything strike you especially as propaganda *in the film?*

This short interchange illustrates the way in which questions become needlessly multiplied only because the initial question does not direct attention to the situation in hand. Here *A* makes a laconic and general observation and the interviewer follows it with a question which merely *implies* a reference to the film under discussion. Without adequate guidance, the interviewee interprets the question as referring to his experience at large, rather than to the film, and reports an impression which he has gained in quite another connection. This requires the interviewer to repeat the substance of his earlier question. From numerous other instances, it can be inferred that the digression and the necessity for a repeated question would both have been avoided had the first question contained an explicit reference to the situation at the focus of interest.

SUBSTANTIVE QUESTIONS, WITH ALLUSION TO THE SITUATION

Not infrequently, the interviewer will want to follow up a statement which is clearly a response to the initial situation. This differs materially from the kind of case which we have just examined in which the interviewee has expressed a general conception and the interviewer is concerned to discover whether this was elicited by the situation. In the present instance, the concern is to have a further elaboration of the situation-related response, and this alone is the reason for the follow-up question. Nevertheless, it seems useful to encourage continued retrospection by incidentally alluding to the situation:

> *A.* . . . The fact of the matter is, if we were sent out green against them [the Nazis], I think we would take a shellacking.
>
> *Int. After seeing this film,* what do you think we are up against when we start invading Europe?

Here the interviewer picks up the essence of the enlisted man's remark which implies a fear of what he will be up against in meeting the enemy. In doing so, he refers to the film which makes it the more likely that the next observation will be linked with the experience of having seen the documentary motion picture.

Again, the interviewer may want to introduce another dimension into the discussion. Appropriate reference to the stimulus situation goes far toward ensuring that this new aspect will be considered in the light of that situation:

> *A.* It was kind of smart that way . . . [the Nazi strategy] was brought out [in the film].
>
> *Int.* Well, after seeing a film like that, how do you think, for example, that their strategy compares with the strategy of our leaders?

Particularly in a group interview, a report which starts out by being genuinely retrospective and explicitly related to the situation under review may easily digress into steadily more irrelevant matters. In the following instance, for example, it is the image of why France fell during the early days of World War II which is at the center of interest:

A. The English figure it out for themselves. If the Germans take the Low Countries then they would go to France. By the process of elimination England is next.
Int. What kind of job did France do during that period, if you think back on the film?

The interviewee is beginning to wander from the subject of the conquest of France and the interviewer tries to have him return to the subject in terms of his response to the documentary film which treated it at length. This results in several detailed reports, but as other interviewees enter the conversation, it tends to become increasingly remote from the stimulus situation of the film.

A. *I heard* something else about the Maginot line. It wasn't so impregnable . . . a lot of the equipment was antiquated.
B. I think France was sold out before Germans marched in because I have heard a lot about that. They had a lot of German people in there and they got their head men to sell them out because after France was captured they found out the truth.

By this point, the interviewer recognizes that interviewees are increasingly going on to report their general attitudes and opinions which were presumably derived from varied sources. Still maintaining the thread of the discussion, he brings them back to report their perceptions of this matter in the film by inserting a casual, but explicit, reference to it:

Int. Now you say France was sold out. *If you stop to think about it, to think back on the events shown in the film, for example,* which do you think was more important, in leading to the fall of France, the fifth columnists or the Nazi military strength?
C. Too much confidence in Marshal Petain, an aged man who didn't have the competence to aid the position. *The film emphasized* that to show how the French with the expressions on their faces, how they were baffled.
D. The people in France didn't know what was going on. They thought they could have held out much longer than what they did. *It showed* sketches at first of the last war.

In short, considerable experience suggests that, in general, the interviewer can assist retrospection by including references, however casual, to the stimulus situation in his follow-up questions, whether the aim is to elicit further details or to re-direct attention to a major theme.

IMPLIED ALLUSION TO STIMULUS

The same results can often be achieved by an *implied* allusion to the original experience, either as a question in itself or as part of a question designed to explore an interviewee's remark further.

When the allusion constitutes a question in itself it is practically the same as the directive questions discussed above, except that the reference to the film is elliptical:

A. I think they signed the pact to give them time to build up because they knew what was coming.

Int. What gave you that idea?

B. That is the way the film showed it, that the Russians knew what was coming from the book *Mein Kampf* and that Hitler hated Russia and wanted the land.

Here the interviewer makes a directive reference to the film situation, and means, in effect: "What *in the film* gave you that idea?" The interviewee catches the implication, and his elaboration is definitely film-related.

Or another example:

A. They wanted to conquer the world.

Int. What gave you that idea?

A. Well, in one part of it there, in the first part, where he was making all those statements that he would rule the world.

In such instances, misunderstandings similar to those pointed out on page 00 might arise, because the interviewee's first statement is general enough to have been based on experience other than the one he has just undergone. However, this subject rightly interprets the interviewer's question as meaning "What *in the film* gave you that idea?" and his answer is definitely film-related.

A second kind of occasion on which an implied allusion to the stimulus situation often proves adequate occurs when the interviewer is following up an idea, but wants to ensure that it is retrospective, not merely introspective, in nature:

> *Int. What kind of propaganda was there, for example, that stood out?*

The use of the past tense here implies "stood out in the film." In this case the interviewer's question was followed by reference to the film, but there is always the possibility that the interviewee may not sense the implication and will instead interpret such a question as referring to his experience at large.

In general, then, when the interviewer wants to have a response linked to the situation, as a prerequisite to specificity, he introduces a direct question: "What gave you that impression?" He is more apt to obtain stimulus-linked specification, however, if he also refers to the salient parts of the stimulus situation in his question: "*What part of the film* gave you that impression?" And by including further references to the interviewee's previously stated response— "What part of the film gave you the impression *that the Nazis are well equipped?*"—he is likely not only to have the response linked to its source, but to prevent unproductive digressions.

In summary, the canon of specificity not only requires the interviewer to ferret out meanings of different phases of the stimulus situation; it also requires him to discover differential responses to the "same" phases of that situation. Differences in predispositions[5] lead subjects to perceive quite

---

5. These variations in predispositions can in turn be linked with the personal contexts of individuals; for an apposite case which relates the predisposing attitude to a pertinent status of the interviewee, see Chapter VI.

different aspects of the same content. Thus, Anglophobes responded to film scenes of the Dunkirk evacuation by seizing solely upon the self-interest of the British:

> The evacuation of Dunkirk showed me that the British *could* do it, if they have to. They showed they could do it and were brave enough to do it *in the case where it was Britain they were fighting for.* They didn't start fighting until they got awful close to home.

But those with favorable or neutral attitudes toward the British noted that some French soldiers were also rescued:

> It shows courage; you mustn't give up. These fellows were practically doomed, and up comes England and salvages them, saves the greatest number of them. The English did a marvelous job . . . fighting their way to the coast, evacuated the whole army *and the French.*

Specific evidence of such selective perception enables the investigator to interpret the occurrence or absence of effects rather than accept these as brute data or resort to conjecture, unbuttressed by evidence.

In general, specifying questions should be explicit enough to aid the interviewee in relating his responses to determinate aspects of the stimulus situation and yet general enough to avoid having the interviewer structure it. This twofold requirement is best met by unstructured questions, which contain explicit references to the situation under review.

CHAPTER V

{ Depth

Depth, as a further criterion of the focused interview, requires reports of affective responses which are elaborated considerably beyond limited, one-dimensional reports of "positive" or "negative," "favorable" or "unfavorable" responses. The interviewer seeks to obtain a maximum of *self-revelatory reports of how the situation under review was experienced.*

The depth of reports in an interview varies; not everything reported is on the same psychological level.[1] The depth of comments may be thought of as varying along a continuum. At the lower end of the scale are mere descriptive accounts of reactions which allow little more than a tabulation of positive or negative responses. At the upper end are those reports which set forth varied psychological dimensions of the experience. In these are expressed symbolisms, anxieties, fears, sentiments, as well as cognitive ideas. A major task of the interviewer, then, is *to diagnose the level of depth on which the interview is proceeding at any particular time and to shift the level toward that end of the "depth-continuum" which he finds appropriate to the given case.*

---

1. See F. J. Roethlisberger and W. J. Dickson, *Management and the Worker,* pp. 276-78.

In general, this involves attempts to achieve greater depth since, as we have often noted, a focused *interview* would be unwarranted if it did not provide more intensive data than those obtainable through the use of such instruments as the questionnaire. Yet, however detailed and circumstantial the reports are, it is evident that the single focused interview, constrained by limitations of time and centered on a particular situation, is not designed to reach the depth commonly attained in the psychoanalytic interview. In the special case of focused interviews of groups, moreover, there are occasions on which the interviewer will find it advisable to shift to a more superficial level in order to obtain comparable data about the responses of a larger number of individuals. This occurs most frequently in those interviews which threaten to be monopolized by one or two members of the group to the virtual exclusion of other interviewees.

Functions of Depth Interviewing

When the interviewer has successfully managed this aspect of the interview, when he has obtained a substantial range of depth responses, he is better equipped to develop hypotheses relating the response to the situation. The exploration of the many-sided and deeply-rooted characteristics of responses enables the interviewer to determine the degree of detachment or of personal involvement in the experience and to evaluate the peripheral or salient character of the responses.

The degree of detachment or of personal involvement is not indicated in a summary expression of preferences. The phrase, "I didn't like . . ." has a variety of possible meanings, none of which is disclosed by this initial designating statement. It may mean that the individual is responding as a "detached critic," and is critically appraising the *presentation* of a document or the development of a social situation from a technical standpoint. He may be responding to a technically defective picture, to what he takes to be monotonous repetition, or to some other technically appraised aspect of the situation. Interesting as these detached observations may be in their own right, they are probably not so much the concern of the interviewer as are the responses which occur with some measure of personal involvement. The responses which indicate that the interviewee was in some way disturbed or otherwise affected by the *content* of the situation are generally of more direct interest for the interviewer. These responses may mean that the situation evoked painful anxieties and fears or that the person felt resentful of what he defines as an effort to "propagandize" him by playing upon his sentiments and values. Without appropriate elaboration of the "don't like" response, the interviewer is confined to uncontrolled conjectures about the social or psychological implications of the response. The canon of depth directs attention to the meanings which constitute the covert significance of otherwise ambiguous or incomplete responses.

The criterion of depth also sensitizes the interviewer to variations in the saliency of responses. Some responses will be central and invested with affect, urgency, or intense feelings; others will be peripheral, of limited significance to the subject. The interviewer must elicit sufficiently detailed data to discriminate the casual expression of an opinion, which is mentioned only because the interview situation seems to call for it, from the strongly motivated response which reaches into central concerns of the informant. It appears that the atmosphere of an expressive interview allows greater opportunity for degrees of saliency to be detected than the self-ratings of intensity of belief which have lately been incorporated into questionnaires and attitude scales. But, unless the interviewer is deliberately seeking out depth responses, he may not obtain the data needed to distinguish the central from the peripheral response.

In cases in which seemingly "detached" responses occur, the interviewer often assumes that these are of only peripheral concern to the interviewee, and, therefore, that they should be by-passed in the search for more significant responses. But it cannot be assumed that seeming *detachment is necessarily synonymous with lack of centrality;* often, further probing reveals a high degree of affective involvement in such seemingly "objective" or "technical" statements as "I think this film didn't go far enough in stressing the anti-Fascist character of the war," "It would do civilians good to see this film," and so on.

In our studies of radio and film "morale propaganda" during World War II, we often encountered one kind of seemingly detached response which, upon further inquiry, turned out to tap deep affective involvement. This took the form of technically-oriented comments containing thinly veiled criticisms of others which, in turn, are seen to be sharp criticisms of self. The following passage from a group interview illustrates this recurrent response:

A. The news is not coming home enough. It should be *forced on people* for the duration.

B. That's the trouble. We don't realize how bad it is. We don't hear enough of it. Things should be brought before the public to *make them, and myself included, more war-conscious.*

Although these two short statements do not in themselves indicate the saliency of the responses, the judgment of insufficient war-consciousness on the homefront is evidently not completely detached. By probing these responses further, it would be possible to check the intimation that although they are apparently criticizing the public at home, these enlisted men are critical of their own failure to feel themselves emotionally involved in events which, in terms of patriotic norms, should be significant to them.

The outer detachment of an initially reported response is not a sufficient basis for taking it to be of only peripheral concern to the interviewee. The interviewer should be prepared to find that, as he shifts the plane of discussion toward greater depth, detachment may give way to personal involvement, apparently peripheral responses may reveal themselves as highly central. This can be put in the form of a working rule for the interviewer: *no response should be considered detached until depth-interviewing has confirmed this inference; no response considered peripheral, until probing has failed to establish it as central.*

Procedures

The criterion of depth requires the interviewee to explore and to report the affective meanings of his responses. It is particularly in point, therefore, that the interviewee, not the interviewer, initiate and develop the components of his response. Above all, *interviewees should continue to be oriented toward the situation under review rather than to the interviewer.* Two general conditions of the interview, which we have briefly considered in other connections, have been found to make for this sustained orientation toward the original situation and therefore merit further consideration here.

FLEXIBILITY OF INTERVIEW SITUATION

When the interviewer focuses wholly on the hypotheses he has developed, he tends to structure the interview in such a way as to delimit the degree of spontaneity of report, and the interview loses that flexibility which makes for self-exploration of feelings. The interviewee becomes increasingly oriented to the interviewer, seeking to infer or to anticipate his expectations. Before long, the interviewee comes to report, with some regularity, that part or aspect of his response which the interviewer apparently invites. When, for instance, the stimulus situation is a news broadcast, this inflexible type of interview commonly elicits standardized

types of report: interviewees define the interview situation
as a test designed to gauge their recollection of facts; they
focus on the details of the news report, the sequence of
specific items of news, and the like. Even when they have
had affective responses toward the content, say, of news about
a disastrous defeat in a battle, the interviewer's focus on
what amounts to a "quiz" on facts vitiates reports of these
responses. The interviewer may assume that he is setting the
stage for later depth-reports by beginning to ask for an
enumeration of the items of news, only to find that he has
established an attitudinal set for coldly factual recollections.
Not infrequently, interviewees focus, not on their affective
experience at the time of hearing the news broadcast, but on
the interviewer-defined task of obtaining "a passing grade"
for accurate memory of facts. Interviews which are crowded
with such questions as "What else do you remember about
the broadcast [film]?" or "Do you remember any other details about that particular part of the broadcast [film]?" often
result in largely neutralizing potentially affective reports of
actual response.

On the other hand, if the interviewer prematurely em-
phasizes his interest in reports of affective response he forces
an inflexible standard upon interviewees which they come to
believe they must meet. This is apt to occur if he seeks to
prime the pump by suggesting types of possible response.
Rather than admit that they are "failures," that they did not
react as they "should have," interviewees may respond to this
by conjuring up reports of responses that never were. Once
again, they are led to orient themselves toward the expectations of the interviewer. They become task-oriented and convert the interview into a test situation.

Both types of procedure lead to a misplaced definition of
the interview situation as an occasion for satisfying the expectations (or even demands) of the interviewer. In reacting
primarily to him rather than reliving the earlier situation,

interviewees are largely shut off from detailing reports of their actual responses: in the one case, depth responses have occurred but are not reported, and in the other, depth responses which have not in fact occurred may be reported.

RETROSPECTIVE FOCUS

It is in this special connection that we reconsider techniques for having interviewees continue to focus their attention on the original situation rather than on the interviewer. The function of retrospection has been discussed at length in Chapter II, but some mention should be made of its particular role in facilitating the report of depth responses.

Occasionally, as we have seen, it requires no more than the reinstatement of the stimulus situation to elicit a detailed account of the response. Consider, for example, the following comment in a group interview:

> *Int.* The next scene shows the raising of the flag [holding up still]. Do you remember this . . . very few of you liked it. What about that part?
> *A.* We liked the flag, but the Navy "E" thing is boring. Why should they get the Navy "E" and all that glory, when they are getting damned big money for it, in my estimation?

> Here the mere reinstatement of a scene at once elicits an expression of attitude. This kind of immediate report apparently occurs when the original situation had evoked a highly affective and articulated response. In such cases, it is probable that almost any reference to the specific situation will elicit the report which is ready for expression.

In most cases, however, responses are neither so well defined nor so definitely formulated that a circumstantial report will follow directly from the re-presentation of the stimulus situation or of a cue to it. More often, the interviewer finds it necessary to assist subjects in their self-exploration or to probe for the responses. Several techniques have been found useful for the purpose of eliciting reports of *affective responses.*

FOCUS ON FEELINGS

In following up comments, the interviewer may call for two types of elaboration. He may ask the subjects to describe *what* they observed in the stimulus situation, thus inviting fairly detached, though significantly selective, accounts of the content. Or he can ask them to report how they *felt* about the content. Both types of elaboration are useful; but the latter more often leads to depth responses. Consequently, in this chapter we sketch only those tactics which lead to the second type of elaboration.

It has been found that interviewees move rather directly toward a report of depth responses when follow-up questions contain key words which refer explicitly to a *feeling context.* Focusing on a fairly recent, concrete experience, interviewees usually become progressively interested in exploring its previously unverbalized dimensions, and, for the most part, no elaborate detour is needed to have them express their sentiments. But the context for such reporting must be established and maintained. Thus the interviewer should phrase a question in such terms as "How did you *feel* when . . . ?" rather than imply a mere mnemonic context by asking "What do you *remember* about . . . ?"

Illustrations are plentiful to show how such seemingly slight differences in phrasing lead respondents from an impersonal description of content to reports of their emotional responses to this content.

> *Int.* Do you happen to remember the scene showing the way Warsaw was being bombed and hit? What stood out about that part of the film?
>
> *A.* The way the people didn't have any shelter; the way they were running around and getting bombed. . . .

The interviewer's "What stood out?" has elicited only an abbreviated account of the objective content of the specific part of the film. He might have proceeded to follow this line of thought—elaborations of the objective events, further details of the squadrons of bombers, and so on. But this would have been comparatively unproductive, since the interviewer is primarily concerned with what these episodes *meant* to the interviewee. He therefore shifts attention to the response level which elicits an elaborate report of feeling, which we reproduce in part.

Int. How did it make you feel when you saw the scenes of the destruction of Warsaw?

B. I still can't get worked up over it yet, because in this country you just can't realize war is like over there. I'm talking for myself. I know I couldn't fight at the present time with the viciousness of one of those people. I could shoot a man before he'd shoot me. But I couldn't have the viciousness I know those people have. . . .

The following passage indicates admirably what happens when the interviewer fails to shift from the level of observation to the level of feeling:

A. *We have better equipment.*

Int. What do you think of their equipment? Did you notice any in the film?

The comment made by *A* followed spontaneously from a discussion of the comparative training given Nazi and American soldiers. This prior context implied that *A* perhaps countered his doubts concerning his readiness for battle by pointing out the superiority of American materiel. Instead of testing this hypothesis, instead of determining the feelings implied in the comparison, the interviewer in effect asks interviewees to act as experts on ordnance and other military equipment.

A. Cheap-looking to me.

Int. Any other ideas? Did you notice any of their equipment you would be apt to remember?

A. Yes, the dive bombers. They didn't have [re]tractable wheels and landing gear. That breaks your speed down and everything.

Int. Did you notice any other equipment?

B. Some of the big bombers looked like they were built like cracker boxes.

The interviewer persists in imposing the role of technical experts upon the group. Having bypassed his first oppor-

tunity for eliciting affective responses, he might still have
determined just what affective overtones are associated with
the observation that Nazi equipment is "cheap." What does
it mean to the enlisted men? Does it lead to a feeling of
complacency? Is it a rationalization? Instead of following
the course, however, the interviewer quizzes his subjects
further concerning their impressions and recollections of
Nazi equipment. The result is that the interviewees accept
the designated role of technical critic and proceed to sketch
out a series of defects.

The essential requirement of techniques designed to
achieve depth, then, is that *they deal, not with objective
content, but with associated feelings.* The interviewer need
not hesitate to make the necessary transition from one level
to the other, for apparently objective observations often
have definite emotional implications. In these circumstances,
the interviewer can be free to "misunderstand" objective
observations, and to focus immediately on associated feelings.

RESTATEMENT OF IMPLIED OR EXPRESSED FEELINGS

Once the context of feelings has been established, further
elaboration will be prompted by occasional restatements of
the feelings implied or expressed. This technique, extensively developed by Carl Rogers in his work in psychothera-
peutic counseling, serves a twofold function. By so rephras-
ing emotionalized attitudes, the interviewer implicitly invites
progressive elaboration by the informant. And, second, such
reformulations enhance rapport, since the interviewer thus
makes it clear that he fully "understands" and "follows" the
informant, as he proceeds to express his feelings.[2]

The first of these functions is evident. When the interviewer repeats expressed feelings, or verbalizes implied ones,
it is clear that he is awaiting an elaboration of the report.
For if he were not interested in hearing more about the mat-

2. Carl Rogers, *Counseling and Psychotherapy,* and "The Non-directive
Method for Social Research," *American Journal of Sociology,* L (1945),
279-83.

ter, he could readily turn the discussion to another subject.

The second function is somewhat less apparent, but probably more important. The restatement of expressed or implied feelings has been found to maintain or deepen rapport with the interviewee since it registers an understanding which is becoming mutual. Without having the interviewer report his own sentiments, the restatement serves as a sign of "acceptance" of the expressed response, and encourages the subject to explore his sentiments even further.

The importance of this function can be appreciated by contrasting the procedure of restatement with other techniques which imply anything but the interviewer's understanding or acceptance of the response. Suppose, for example, that the interviewer replies by directly denying or challenging the interviewee's expression of a sentiment. The process of self-exploration is brought to an abrupt halt. The interviewee is no longer engaged in developing his report but finds himself, instead, placed in the position of trying to defend his response by "objective proof," or of trying to gain the interviewer's assent by tentatively putting out alternative opinions with which the interviewer might agree. In either case, the interviewee is not only blocked from further self-exploration, but turns his attention from the stimulus situation itself to the demands of the interviewer. This is scarcely calculated to result in detailed accounts of depth responses.

Or again, the interviewer may reply by asking for further clarification of the expressed sentiment—"What do you mean by that?" or "Could you explain that a little better?" Although questions such as these imply the interviewer's interest in further description of the response, they tend to stand in the way of such elaboration. The interviewer's failure to understand the initial remark, a failure which may be genuine or tactical, is generally taken to mean that the interviewee is being asked to explain his response *on the*

same plane of depth which characterized the original report.
Instead of exploring his feelings further, he tends to reiterate his previous remarks or to offer evidence in their
support.

The manner in which the restatement of implied feelings
facilitates self-exploration and the elaboration of affective
responses is illustrated in the following passage:

> *Int.* How about some of the rest of you on that? We have
> had men tell us over and over again that they like
> action shots in films. Now, what we are trying to find
> out is why? What do you get out of it?
> *A.* You build up morale. It is a morale builder. *It is like
> waving a red flag in front of a bull.*
> *Int. You find yourself getting mad?*
> *B. You can't help it,* sitting there as a red-blooded Ameri-
> can, *and see some war lord overrunning women and
> children.* Most of the fellows or a good percentage are
> married and left children at home while serving in the
> Army.

There is, of course, such a thing as the social correctness
of displayed emotion, and interviewees, in the distance of
retrospection, may accordingly censor their self-reports, denying (sometimes, even to themselves) the stirrings of sentiment. The mood of emotional responsiveness called forth by
the stimulus situation may have been replaced, in the in-
terim, by a socially more acceptable prudence. The dry-eyed
report may unwittingly or perhaps deliberately omit any
reference to the actually experienced feelings. The original
experience, recollected in tranquillity, may be presented as
having itself been tranquil.

In the group interview, or before rapport has been thoroughly established in a solo interview, when a report is a
projective account of painful or socially unacceptable feelings, the interviewer will generally *not* facilitate depth responses by restating those feelings with *direct* reference to
the person who expressed them. More often than not, this
has the effect of blocking the subject: he may feel that he

has been trapped into an uncomfortable admission, or made to reveal sentiments which he prefers not to be made public. There may emerge in retrospect a sense of shame inhibiting further report when, removed from the situation itself, the person feels his response to have been excessive, or unmanly, or sentimental. In such cases, the interviewee will often dry up the report of his experience by retreating into generalities and impersonal statements which remove from him the responsibility for the expressed feelings.

The interviewer can avoid this kind of retreat and facilitate depth by so phrasing his restatement that his interest in and understanding of the original statement refers to the general type of implied response, rather than to an idiosyncratic (and possibly "excessive") response. In the group interview, this means that the question will be *extensive in reference:* "Have *any of you* ever had the feeling that . . . ?" In the individual interview, the functionally comparable question will be *projective: "Someone* might feel that . . . ?" In this way the interviewee is encouraged to elaborate his response and to explore his feelings without being required to "admit" to them before he is ready to do so. The problem then remains, of course, to learn whether the statements actually refer to "other people" rather than to self or are simply a cloak for his own, not yet admitted, feelings. The problem lends itself to solution by having the interviewee continue his report of experience, for as he reports the affect stirred by the situation, he tends, sooner or later, to provide bases for distinguishing between the two.

In the following example, a *restatement of feelings* moves from the general to the particular and though this does not lead the interviewee to acknowledge openly that the fear response is his own, it does help him localize the nature of the response.

> *A.* Well, some of the boys in service should not see scenes of destruction and things like that. Even though they are men, *it will put a fear in them.* I think either *it will*

> *make them more afraid to go in there,* or it would make
> them mad. Of course, it depends upon the disposition
> of the person, what he is made of.

Int. Did *any of you* feel this at any part of the film—*"Well,*
by gosh, if this is the kind of thing I have to face, I pre-
fer not to?"

A. Yes, because *I know some of them* will feel that way,
but I believe the average person won't . . . and I do
think that *those that do feel that they couldn't take it—*
well, before they get through their training they will get
to feeling that way too.

The restatement of expressed or implied feelings serves as
a "continuant remark" which invites the fuller reporting of
depth responses. It is more useful than other types of continuant remarks—e.g., "What do you mean?" "Could you tell
me a little more about that?"—since it affords evidence that
the interviewer *has* understood the response of the interviewee and thinks it of sufficient interest to have it described
at greater length. The give-and-take of social interaction is
maintained in this way, and the interviewee is ordinarily
encouraged to explore his feelings further rather than to
remain on the same plane of depth.

COMPARATIVE SITUATIONS

In certain cases the interviewer can use the partially directive technique of suggesting comparisons between the
situation under review and parallel experiences which the
subjects are known or can be presumed, to have had. Such
comparisons of concrete experiences serve to encourage
depth responses by providing a bridge to those critical areas
in which there is reason to believe that affective responses
have occurred. They aid the verbalization of affect. Drawing
parallels (or contrasts) between the indicated situation and
other experiences affords interviewees an opportunity to talk
more readily about their anxieties, fears, and other affects;
to tell of terrifying or emotionally charged experiences in
the relatively distant past is not to confess current "weak-

nesses," and once this pattern of acknowledging one's feelings is established, it tends to persist. In short, the suggested comparison is designed not to have interviewees draw objective parallels or contrasts between experiences, but to serve as a release for introspective and affective responses.

Witness the following excerpt from an interview with inductees into the army, who had implied that they were watching a documentary film about Nazi military training in the light of their own training experience. For these men, the training of Nazis could be presumed to be something more than a matter of casual interest for these were, in prospect, the very kinds of soldiers they would be facing in combat. By starting with a comparison of Nazi and American types of military training, the interviewer provides a springboard from the film to the meanings which the film has held for them.

> *Int.* Do you suppose that we Americans train our men in the same way [i.e., comparison with Nazi training as shown in the film]?
> *A.* They train them more thoroughly.
> *B.* The way things are rushed through our training over here, it doesn't seem possible.
> *C.* That's what enters my mind about the training we are getting here. Of course, a lot of talk exists among the fellows that as soon as training is over, we're going into the fight. I don't know any more about it than they do. The training we're going to get right here is just our basic training, and if we get shipped across, *I can't see that we'd know anything about it except marching and doing a little left and right flank and a few things like that.* . . .

The suggested comparison provided an apt occasion for these soldiers to go on to express their anxieties about going overseas inadequately prepared for combat. The nominally objective comparison of affectively significant episodes elicited an open expression of feelings and meanings. The interviewer was then able to ascertain the specific scenes in the film which had activated these anxieties.

The characteristic efficacy of this technique of comparison can be further glimpsed by considering a similar occasion on which it was not used. In this case, the interviewer focuses on the objective content of the film without attempting to relate it to parallel experiences of the interviewees. The passage is taken from a group interview with recruits who were being trained as engineers:

> *Int.* Well, we were talking about the training of the Nazi groups a minute ago. Do you happen to remember anything that gave you a slant on how well trained their troops are or how poorly trained?
>
> *A.* In my estimation, they are well trained—you take the *engineers,* for instance, building up bridges and going down embankments.
>
> *B.* Attack on the Maginot Line.
>
> *C.* It looked to me like a hardship to march like they do because *I know we march here free and easy* and it gets to be tiresome after a while, and that is an unnatural position in my estimation. Why do they do things like that?
>
> *B.* That is part of their regimentation. It looks nice.

One defect in the wording of the interviewer's question has been examined in our review of questions which center on matters of memory: "Do you remember . . . ?" Moreover, as the italicized portions of the replies indicate, these soldiers had perceived themselves as counterparts of the enemy soldiers and were poised to make affectively significant comparisons. The interviewer neglects this cue with the result that the comments are confined to estimates of the training of the enemy; nothing is reported about the affective meanings of all this.

It should be emphasized, however, that the indiscriminate use of comparisons will not effectively release depth responses. To be effective, the experience drawn upon for comparison must itself be centrally significant to the interviewee. If this is not recognized, if the interviewer introduces comparisons with abstract problems or with peripheral experiences, he will find that this procedure, far from facilitating reports of depth responses, actually disrupts the continuity of the interview. It imposes an alien frame of reference upon the interviewee. In such instances, the interviewer often becomes a target for hostility: he is asked to define his terms, to state the purpose of his question, to defend his behavior. This is the first skirmish in what can develop into a rousing battle, as the interviewer is called upon to explain himself. Consider, once again, this passage from an interview with a group of army trainees (which has been considered at some length in Chapter III) :

> *Int.* How do you suppose—now that you think back on the picture—how do you suppose the Nazi strategy compares with the strategy of the Allied leaders?

"Strategy" is an abstract concept with which these rank-and-file soldiers can scarcely have had much to do. What is more, the earlier parts of the interview had not considered matters of strategy at all. The requested comparison is defined by these privates as a difficult and extraneous task: they are being called upon to reflect and to report on complex problems remote from their own role and experience. The result is general confusion as interviewees grope for further cues and cross-examine the interviewer.

> *A.* Are you including all the world in that now?
> *Int.* Yes.
> *B.* At the present or at that time?
> *Int.* Well, at that time, first.

These and other questions of like kind serve notice on the interviewer that he has succeeded only in stirring up confusion and in arousing the hostility of the ill-oriented soldiers. But committed to an interviewing tactic, however misplaced, he persists in opening wider the Pandora's box of abstract and irrelevant comparison. He tries again:

> *Int.* How would you compare the planning they showed there with our planning in North Africa? Which do you think was better?
> *C.* You say our planning in Africa? *I haven't seen any.*
> *Int.* What do you mean?

C. They show the diagrams on the screen how the Germans went into France or captured Poland or Norway, but as far as Africa, I mean fighting towards . . . away from . . . Tunisia, *I don't know.*

A. *I don't think you can compare them* because they are all in different positions, not in the same countries.

By now, the interviewer is completely routed. This badly advised comparison has not only failed to elicit reports of depth responses but has produced an atmosphere hardly conducive to such reports later in the interview.

The comparison of the situation under review with other situations is patently a two-edged tool, to be used with caution and in the proper direction. To encourage reports of feelings, the situation selected for comparison should have entered significantly into the interviewee's prior experience. It is different with abstract or obscure comparisons which divert attention from the relevant, arouse the hostility of the interviewee and, altogether, have nothing to recommend them.

SUMMARY

The depth of reported responses varies from the superficial indication of affective attitudes, the mere statement of "like" or "dislike," to expressive and detailed accounts of the feelings aroused by the stimulus situation. To a considerable extent, the interviewer can control the shifting planes of depth: he can so canalize the discussion as to reach greater or lesser depth.

Several procedures can be used to shift the report from one plane to another. The first of these involves an *allusion to feelings* evoked by the situation rather than a request for objective observations about the situation: "How did you *feel* when you say (heard) . . . ?" A second procedure is appropriate only when a report of feelings has been initiated. This requires the *restatement, either direct or implied, of feelings* which have been explicitly reported or intimated.

The function of such restatements for maintaining or enlarging rapport in the interview has been considered in some detail. A third procedure involves a directed *comparison between the situation in hand and other significant experiences which the interviewer knows or has reason to assume have been central for the interviewee.* As we have just seen, such comparisons, when properly used, help interviewees to tell of affective responses which are otherwise beyond their powers to report. This, however, is as potentially dangerous as it is potentially useful. When the comparison is with matters abstract or peripheral, the interview is often thrown into confusion. It is therefore unwise to introduce comparison unless there is some assurance that it is concrete, relevant and central.

CHAPTER VI } Personal Contexts

The Concept of Personal Context[1]

To arrive at an understanding of definitions of a situation, and responses to it, the focused interview is designed to discover what each person has imported into the situation. The person's prior attitudes and values and certain of his social statuses and roles constitute the personal context of his responses. It is the variation in personal context which leads to variations in response to the same type of situation by the same individual at different times or by different individuals at the same time. This is not to deny, in advance, that there may nevertheless occur a modal response which is characteristic of those having pertinent similarities of personal context. The more nearly adequate the knowledge of these contexts, the more nearly one can account for the meanings which the individual has assigned to the situation.

The search for depth responses and for personal contexts are closely related, but distinguishable. In ascertaining depth responses, the interviewer tries to identify the affective meanings of the particular experience; in ascertaining personal context, he tries to discover the attributes of the individual which have imbued this experience with these

---

1. Cf. Roethlisberger and Dickson, *Management and the Worker,* pp. 273-283.

meanings. Frequently, the same procedures will elicit the two related kinds of data.

Types of Context

Two kinds of personal context can be usefully distinguished. The first of these, the *idiosyncratic context,* refers to those highly personal experiences and associated attitudes which occur rarely even within a relatively homogeneous group. For an example, the American who says of a documentary radio program: ". . . it reminds me of the way I felt when my brother came back from the war after he had been reported dead. We were living in Russia and . . ." An idiosyncratic context shapes responses to a situation which are apt to be distinctive if not actually unique and helps explain what might otherwise appear to be a response wholly disproportionate to the occasion.

The second type is the *role context* which is built up of experiences which are common among persons occupying a particular social status. The role context helps account for relatively frequent, if not actually modal, responses to a situation. In the excerpt that follows, for example, it is the interviewee's status as a soldier which is linked with his response to a sequence of scenes in a documentary film:

> *Int.* Do you happen to remember what you didn't like about that part about the WAACS?
> *A.* I'll tell you the truth. I don't go in to see Army routines. *I see too much of it.* I think they should get rid of that entirely. I don't think it is interesting to *anybody.*

In concluding the account of his own response, this interviewee promptly assumes it to be a prevailing, if not exclusive, response and ascribes it to everyone. This has been found to be a fairly common practice: the interviewee will explicitly place his response in its role context and then, abandoning the sociological force of his own observation, assume that it occurs quite apart from this context. *Sus-*

tained recognition of role contexts by those involved in them seems to be difficult and infrequent.

The purposes of his study, of course, govern the interviewer's primary concern with one or the other of the two types of personal context. In studying the effects of mass communications, for example, the interviewer will probably have only slight interest in idiosyncratic contexts which cannot account for widespread patterns of response. As a contrasting example, interviews focused on the diaries of medical students who have distinguished themselves from their fellows in one or another respect will be as much concerned with the idiosyncratic as with the role context.

Relevance of Personal Contexts

It is a central task of the focused interview to learn how the prior experiences and dispositions of interviewees are related to their structuring of the stimulus situation. As we consider the matter in some detail, it will be seen that personal contexts clarify every phase of the engagement of persons in situations.

What is perceived in the situation, the meanings ascribed to it, vary largely as the personal context varies. Particularly when exposed to complex and ongoing events, people orient themselves in terms of highly selective perceptions. It is a function of the interview to bring these into focus and to have them related, at least hypothetically, to the personal contexts of perception.

It is particularly for the understanding of the unanticipated response that knowledge of personal context becomes conspicuously essential. For the response *is* unanticipated precisely because there seems to be nothing in the objective situation to provide substance for this kind of interpretation or reaction. In behavior elicited by communications, this often takes the form of what has been described as the "boomerang response," that is, a response which is directly opposed to the intent or expectation of those issuing the communication (whether these be the producers of mass communications in print, radio, television, and motion pictures or the producers of private communications in and out of organizations). Typically, the response is anything but unexpected, once the personal context of response is identified and taken into account.

Consider the following boomerang response, which is taken from an interview with trainees who had seen a documentary film concerning the early stages of the recent world war. The film has stressed the strength, efficiency and military superiority of the Nazis over other European countries and had dramatically portrayed the valiant resistance of the British against what were then seemingly overwhelming odds.

Int. What kind of a fighting job do you think the British did during the period shown in the film?

A. Not any more than they ever did. [This devaluation of the British war effort comes as something of a surprise, in view of the circumstantial account to the contrary in the documentary film. But the interviewee at once supplies the context which explains his response.] *I am just Irish enough to believe Britain will never fight if they can get somebody else to go to the front for them.* . . . You hear talk that they will fight to the last Canadian and last Scotchman, and they will. There is no question about it. . . . [To this point, he simply reports his status-linked attitude toward the British without connecting this with the film. It soon turns out, however, that he was not simply impervious to the story which the film tells, but has selectively seen in it only that which confirms his attitude.] *What did you see in the film that England did outside of evacuating at Dunkirk?*

The focused interview results in an inventory of personal contexts found to govern responses to a particular type of situation. It then remains for other research procedures to estimate or to find out the relative frequency with which each of these contexts obtain among those exposed to the situation, either experimentally or routinely in their patterns of social life.

As we have briefly suggested in the preceding chapter and shall consider at length in this one, interviewees are often reluctant to express their most deeply felt emotions. Yet the social protocol of the interview situation ordinarily requires them "to say something." As a defensive maneuver, which is nonetheless a maneuver when it is unwitting, they may resort to impersonal generalities rather than "expose" their genuine feelings. The manifest content of what they report serves only to disguise the substance of their actual response. By progressively shifting the discussion to matters of personal context, the interviewer can provide graduated transitions to the type of report which is being temporarily held in abeyance.

Procedures

Although there is nothing here of a tested recipe guaranteeing that personal contexts will be elicited, several procedures have been found relatively effective for the purpose.

IDENTIFICATION

The interviewer can assume, with some confidence, that people engaging in a social situation or watching it unfold, as in a play, variously experience some measure of social and psychological distance or intimacy between themselves and others in the situation. They may identify themselves with some, feel alienated from others and fail to respond at all to the rest. By focusing on those in the situation with whom the interviewee has identified himself, the interviewer helps the detailed reporting of the personal contexts of response to the situation.

Some degree of previous knowledge about the social and personal attributes of the interviewee provides one source for making hypotheses of probable bases of identifications. At times, such information is ready to hand: a fat woman is found to be particularly concerned to buy her war bonds from Kate Smith; American soldiers training to be engineers have functional bases for identification with German engineering corps depicted in a documentary film. With such provisional guideposts to possible identifications, the interviewer can direct his questions accordingly, probing for the reminiscences of personal experience and of interests activated by this aspect of the situation. When even this modicum of knowledge about potential bases for identification is absent, one must wait upon cues which turn up in the course of the interview.

On occasion, the problem of uncovering identifications solves itself. Without any prompting, the interviewee may spontaneously and explicitly report the grounds on which he has identified himself with one or another person or group in the situation under review. Consider this case in point.[2] During the last war, a radio star, Kate Smith, broadcast over a span of eighteen consecutive hours repeated appeals for the purchase of war bonds. Miss Smith was characteristically described by listeners as a large, stout woman who neither possesses nor makes any apparent effort to achieve sexual allure. In affectionate summary, "she's just fat, plain Kate Smith." A thirty-year-old mother, whose obesity became pronounced after the birth of her second child, is quick to identify herself with Miss Smith and to dissociate herself from more glamorous public figures:

> Take some of these actresses, do they care about anything but themselves? Many of these actresses are beautiful, lovely figures, but *Kate Smith hasn't any of this.* To her, beauty isn't everything. She's just herself. [And further] *I look on*

2. See R. K. Merton, M. Fiske and A. Curtis, *Mass Persuasion* (New York: Harper, 1946), pp. 146-147.

this as a mother: I don't want beauty. Perhaps at sixteen I wanted it, or at nineteen, but now I don't want it any more. [In agitated tones] I'm thinking of my children, I'm not thinking of glamour [this said with withering contempt].

In the following case, it becomes evident that the social class of the interviewee provided the context for heightened identification with the British portrayal in a documentary film:

[The interviewee has said that he "feels closer" to the British, after seeing the documentary film.]
Int. In what way does this picture make you feel closer?
A. I don't come from such a well-to-do family as Mrs. Miniver's. Hers was a well-to-do family and that picture didn't show anything of the poor families. But *this one brought it closer to my class of people,* and you realize we are all in it and everybody gets hurt and not just the higher class of people.

Here is an example of an identification, of such direct import for the interviewee, that even an inept question by the interviewer is enough to bring it to the surface. The following response is to a wartime radio program designed to improve civilian morale:

Int. What about the humor—the stay-at-homes, flat feet, teeth, etc. Did it make the radio program more effective?
A. I don't think it's funny because *I was personally rejected* for the Army and I don't think it was worth being rejected for and that isn't humorous to me.

Despite the interviewer's inadvisable use of a "consultant" question, casting the interviewee in the role of an expert adviser, he indicates a boomerang response, based on his own experience and status as one rejected by the Army.

In other instances, the basis of identification is *spontaneously mentioned,* but the identification is at first *implicit.* The following example is drawn from an interview with a group of Army engineers:

Int. What in the film gave you the idea that the Nazis were well trained?

A. The *engineers* had a bridge across that place—don't know where it was—they had a bridge and those tanks came across it. That is co-operation.

Here one man refers to a part of the film which might well have led him to identify himself with others of like kind. The allusion to engineers is still only a tentative cue: nothing has been said in so many words about the personal context of the observation.

Int. That is an idea. You are fighting *engineers,* aren't you? At least you are engineers-to-be. When you were watching those scenes of the Nazi engineers in action, *what did you find yourselves thinking about?*

The interviewer adapts *A*'s allusion to status to serve as a transition from impersonal observations to personal contexts. To further this shift of focus, he *underlines the attribute on the basis of which the identification is anticipated.* Moreover, the interviewer phrases the question extensively so that others in the group are encouraged to report any responses they may have had within this context.

B. *We would be in soon.*

C. *Hoping the war would be over right away.*

Int. Why? Seriously, that is interesting—why?

However, personal contexts of response have not yet been established. The remark by *C* is particularly ambiguous. Is he anxious over his own fate in battle? Is he simply fed up with army life? The interviewer attempts to determine the context of the response by asking "why?" This abrupt and vague query defeats the interviewer's purpose as *C* replies in as oblique a fashion as before.

C. Just a funny feeling, I guess. Bombs going all around. . . .

Int. *How about some of the rest of you on that?* What did you start thinking about when you saw those scenes of the Nazi engineers building bridges?

A. Makes you think you are going to build a bridge.

D. *About what we would be doing.* Look it over as much as we could and see what it would be like.

> *Int.* How did you feel when you were thinking about that?

The significance of the identification for these two soldiers remains unclarified. They might have been responding, for example, merely to the training technique of the enemy as technical information or, again, they might be indirectly expressing anxieties in anticipation of being called upon to perform the pictured tasks. The interviewer therefore asks for clarification of the response.

> *D.* I believe it said something about the *engineers being first.* I always heard the Marines were the first ones.

Since identifications ordinarily invite accounts of the personal contexts of response, the interviewer does well to be alerted to the spontaneous mention of elements in the situation with which interviewees seem to be identifying themselves. He can then take these cues, and moving from the plane of impersonal or objective discourse, test out his hypothesis of identification by turning to the implied personal context of the response. This can often be done by *emphasizing the implied relation between the interviewee and the relevant aspect of the situation* and, *once having instituted the personal context,* by asking for reports of thoughts and feelings evoked by that aspect of the situation.

At times, the interviewer does well to introduce a tentatively assumed *basis* for identification on his own initiative, when it has not been spontaneously mentioned by the interviewee. When sparingly used, this practice does not seem to produce spurious reports. Experience has shown that the suggested identifications are generally repudiated or ignored by interviewees when they have not in fact occurred.

This procedure should not take the place of efforts to elicit spontaneous statements of identification from the interviewees themselves. But as the interview draws toward a close, with nothing by way of identification having been spontaneously reported, it can be assumed that the discussion will not suffer from a directed shift in focus toward personal references of this kind. The following extract from an interview with another group who had seen the same orientation film includes some interviewing techniques which are effective and others which are ineffective in eliciting personal contexts.

> *Int. You are all fighting engineers. . . .* Do you remember those action shots showing the engineers really at work?

The interviewer supplies a cue to possible identification. But instead of using this as a means of eliciting personal contexts, he, in effect, asks for *proof that the interviewees remember the scenes he has in mind.* This results, at best, in an enumeration of objective details of the episode. Witness the comment.

> *A.* Blew the lock house up and dynamited the place just right.
> *Int.* That is what I would like to find out. While you were watching those scenes showing the Nazi engineers at work, what did you find yourselves thinking about?

This is the type of question which might well have been asked at the outset. It is generally safe to assume that interviewees will remember those scenes which most closely touch on their own past or anticipated experiences. In general, it seems advisable to ask immediately for introspective reports. When attention is centered upon the objective nature of the situation, it becomes difficult thereafter to elicit reports of personal context. The question introduced at this point is largely ineffective.

> *B. We will be doing the same thing* two months from now.
> *Int.* What do you mean—doing as well or what?

This "continuant remark," expressing an inability to understand the comment in the hope that it will be expanded, is of the type which is usually helpful in eliciting an appropriate elaboration of the report.

> *B.* I figured we would be in action two months from now and doing the same thing as they are.
> *C.* I figured some day we would be facing the very thing as those fellows who were building the bridges.
> *Int.* What about that—suppose you were facing it?
> *C.* We would find out who the super race would be— Germany or us.

These few passages from interviews bring out particulars of some rules of thumb to guide the interviewer in cases where interviewees make no spontaneous mention of persons or groups in the situation with which they have identified themselves. In the first place, *the interviewer should preferably provide his cues to the hypothesized identification at points in the interview where they readily follow from the preceding discussion.* As we have seen, there is often considerable resistance to reporting deeply personal contexts of response; this resistance is only reinforced when the interviewer makes it evident, by an abrupt shift of subject, that this is precisely the kind of intimate information which he seeks.

Secondly, *it seems advisable for the interviewer to limit himself to cues, to intimated identifications, rather than to state these expressly.* If identification has occurred, the cue will often be enough to invite the report; if it has not occurred, the cue will generally be insufficient to suggest a pseudo-identification. Moreover, there will be no occasion for people to infer that they have "failed" in their role as interviewees by not having supplied information which is now being requested.

Lastly, *questions should preferably call for introspective reports of the personal attributes or experiences underlying identification rather than for evidence that the pertinent elements of the stimulus situation were remembered.* The preferred procedure makes the transition by such questions as, "You remember those scenes of the Nazi engineers in that part of the film, don't you? What did you *American* engineers find yourselves thinking about when you saw those action shots?" The question focuses on the elements in the situation which may have led to identification and proceeds at once to ask for a report of responses to it.

CONTROLLED PROJECTION

We have seen briefly how the procedures of controlled projection can serve to encourage the reporting of affective and value-laden responses; we consider now how it can be adapted to uncover the personal context of such responses. As interviewees approach spheres of tension which they regard as distinctively personal, they often attribute their own feelings to others. This practice can be drawn upon by the interviewer to elicit detailed accounts of responses at first imputed to, say, the "other guy," "people," or "men in the Army." Since these responses are assigned to others, the otherwise resistant interviewee is ready to elaborate the nature of the responses at some length. He maintains anonymity while engaged in self-exploration of feelings.[3]

It is in the next phase that the projection becomes "controlled" by the interviewer who does not allow the discussion to remain on this level. The person who projects his own affective response onto the generality of men ordinarily senses what he is about, even though he may be hard put to formulate the process or to acknowledge the fact. The initial elaboration of the response does provide an enlarged basis for experiencing the pertinence to himself of the response which he attributes to others. It is for the interviewer to provide the setting in which this can be brought to the surface and put into words. The shift from the level of projection to the level of personal context should not, of course, be sudden and forced. Unless there is evidence of considerable resistance on the part of the interviewee, the interviewer can achieve his purpose by slight, but continued, guidance in this direction.

In the first phase, the projective statements may be introduced either by the interviewer or by the interviewee himself. Here is an example of the way in which the interviewer provides a basis for projection which can easily lead interviewees to report the personal context of their own response. The stimulus situation is one in a series of radio programs

---

3. For some apposite evidence on this, see the summary by Maccoby and Maccoby, "The interview: a tool of social science," *op. cit.*, pp. 460-462.

broadcast during the war for the purpose of heightening the morale of civilians:

> *Int.* Do you think it makes a difference if you have some one in the service when you listen to this program?
>
> *A.* Yes, you think if he is going through that too.
>
> *Int.* Do you think it makes a difference, Mrs. B?
>
> *B.* I have no one in the service so it really doesn't upset me.
>
> *A.* Before my husband went overseas I wasn't much interested in that type of program, but *now that he is overseas I like to listen.*

> *A.* I think we should have more programs like this. There are too many people that are self-satisfied. I would feel terrible if I lost my husband, but at least I would feel. . . .

The interviewer's first query is projective and hypothetical, designed to see if those whom the shoe fits will put it on. There is nothing here, in this group interview, of probing directly into personal concerns. At first, this only elicits the opinion that people in the hypothetical situation will respond distinctively. The interviewer proceeds, in effect, to reiterate the projective question, extending it to other members of the group. This leads to several indications of personal context, and *A* begins to explore the distinctive meanings which the broadcast holds for her.

In other cases, the projective statement may be introduced by the interviewee. This signals the interviewer that the interviewee may be touching upon a sphere of private tension and is initially reluctant to acknowledge this sensitive matter. Acting as an ally of the interviewee, the interviewer proceeds *to focus on the substantive content of the statement. At the same time, he assumes, in his follow-up question, that the interviewee is speaking of himself and makes the translation in an evident mood of acceptance and interest.* By turning to the content of the initial projection, the interviewer implies that he is not engaged in having the interviewee commit himself to the response which has been reported. By incidentally directing his question to the feelings of the interviewee himself, the interviewer is, however, moving from "they" to "I." In cases of relatively slight tension, a single follow-up question of this kind will be sufficient to elicit the personal context. In other, more tension-laden cases, the interviewee will continue to report in projective terms. By sustaining the discussion of the nature of the response, the interviewer can make it possible for the interviewee to refer eventually to his own experience and his own situation.

An example of the spontaneous introduction of a projective response is contained in the following section from a group interview with Army trainees:

> *A.* How about *a man* being interested in *a picture,* but not liking it? It might rub *him* the wrong way, even though *he* finds himself interested in it.

This initial remark seems doubly removed from the personal experience of the soldier who makes it. It refers, in a possibly projective fashion, to "a man" and continues by referring to an undesignated picture. The interviewer converts both general items into specific and personal terms.

Int. Do *you* have *a particular film* in mind?

The question has two functions. First, it directs attention to a specific stimulus situation. Second, it provides an innocuous means of turning the interviewee toward introspection: there is little exposure of self-feelings in identifying the film which arouses the uncomfortable responses mentioned in the original statement. In effect, the interviewer is beginning to test his working hypothesis that this generalized remark is in fact the expression of a personal experience which the soldier hesitates to acknowledge to others (and perhaps to himself). The reply begins to provide evidence in support of the hypothesis, as the soldier begins to report his *own* experience and feelings.

> *A.* That part where they showed some of the wounded soldiers there on Bataan. *I don't care to see that kind*

of stuff, although it was interesting in a way. From the point of view that I haven't seen any actual battle conditions where you see what happens. *I don't care to see pictures like that.*

Int. Why not?

A. I don't know. *It is just a matter of emotions.* My feelings don't press towards that side of films.

Int. It rubs you the wrong way? It irritates you?

The direct, even abrupt, query, "Why not?" is misplaced, and puts the interviewee on the defensive. He retreats into repetition. Aware that he has pressed too rapidly, the interviewer takes a phrase from the subject's original statement, to reassure the interviewee by retracing the steps that have already been covered.

A. No, it's just that I don't know how to express it. It's emotional.

Int. Well, if you think back to the time you were watching, what were your feelings?

A. *I felt that it was a sort of gruesome part of the film.*

To this point, the interviewee has been led from the projective statement that "a picture" might "rub a man the wrong way" to the disclosure that he himself was disturbed by the scenes of wounded Americans on Bataan.

Int. You mean this scene here [holding up still picture]?

The interviewer has identified at least one specific reference of the interviewee's original statement. By continued probing, he attempts to determine the affective components and personal contexts of the response.

B. It seems unnecessary to you?

A. Yes, something like that. *The public* might have a reaction to that if they were exposed to it. Although some of them realize the fact that under battle conditions men must lose their lives or be wounded. *Some people* would say, "Look at that," and it would lower their morale.

C. The main thing was, I think, that *most of the fellows* get a realization that *it might be them.*

Although two of the soldiers refuse to acknowledge their own fears, reverting to generalized projective statements, the door has been opened for *C* to report the anxieties current in the group.

This passage illustrates some of the problems involved in dealing with projective statements. There is no hard and fast rule for assuming that the interviewee refers to himself when he ostensibly talks about others. It is therefore expedient to adopt as a loosely-held working hypothesis, subject to preliminary tests, the assumption *that any responses attributed to others are a projection of the interviewee's own responses.* If the test probes are noncommittal, there need be no loss of rapport in the interview when the evidence subsequently indicates that there was little or nothing of personal response in the seemingly projective comment.

As a general rule, also, it is advisable to pick up, for further discussion, any allusion by interviewees to a social status or category in which they themselves are found. Such allusions often indicate their own perspective on the situation. In the following excerpt from an interview with Negro troops, for example, it soon becomes evident that a training film has stirred sentiments altogether different from those of white troops who had seen the same film.

> *Int.* Was there *anything left out* that you would like to see in other pictures of this type?
> *A.* I would like to see more pictures about the *training of colored soldiers and what they are doing. . . .*

As soon as the social category of "colored troops" is introduced in reply to his open-ended question, the interviewer at once fixes the attention of the group on this context.

> *Int.* Was there any part of this film where you felt it would be better to show something about colored soldiers?
> *B.* *Where it is mixed in, we don't feel that we are segregated.* You never see any of our own activities.
> *C.* *They drafted us the same as they drafted them.*

The array of expressions of sentiments touched off by this query indicate a social context which is highly salient for perception.

By and large, controlled projection provides both interviewer and interviewee with a convenient device for entering upon and exploring responses that are imbued with tension and often resistant to free expression. It is well to remember, however, that this is only a tool and not an end in itself. When a phase of the interview is developing on the plane of seeming projections, when responses to the situation in hand are being attributed to "people" (in general) or to an unidentified "them," the interviewer shifts to the plane of personal reference. In some instances, it will turn out that the report is indeed that of an informant describing the responses of others, rather than that of an interviewee describing his own responses. Even so, the tool will have served to root the report in personal experience which is, after all, the major source of observations for both informant and interviewee.

PARALLELING OF EXPERIENCE

Just as the drawing of comparisons between the situation under review and of other situations has been found useful in eliciting reports of depth responses, so it can be useful, on occasion, in obtaining reports of personal context, when these have not been obtained by the use of identification or of controlled projection.

The paralleling of experiences differs from identification in that the interviewee does not, at the time, consider that it is almost as though he himself were engaged in the situation. It differs from projection in that he acknowledges from the first that the experience is his own. In the use of this procedure, *the interviewee is being led, in effect, to clarify the nature of his response and to establish its personal context by reflecting on comparable experiences in his life history.*

To make use of this procedure, it is ordinarily necessary to put direct questions to the interviewee, asking him to search out his most nearly comparable experience. We note here, as we have noted briefly before, that this procedure is therefore better confined to those interview situations in which considerable rapport has been developed. Such questions as, "Can you give me an example of that from your own experience?," "Does that remind you of anything in your own life?," or "Does that strike a familiar chord?" can readily be taken to "pry" into essentially private affairs and evoke resistance rather than response.

Where interview conditions are suitable, however, requests for parallel experiences in the life of interviewees greatly aid the reporting of personal contexts of response. In the following example from an interview with a woman who bought a war bond from Kate Smith, the interviewer does not introduce his request for a parallel experience until he has found that other types of inquiry fail to elicit a report of personal context:

A. The others don't make too much of an impression on me.

Int. What's the difference?

A. . . . She hit deep . . . she was real, she meant it, she stated true facts in a down-to-earth way.

Int. How do you mean—can you give me an example?

A. . . . her voice . . . the way she spoke . . . she didn't ask you to buy bonds . . . she doesn't *tell* you all that, you *feel* all that.

Int. How do you think she does it—*can you think of something in your own life* that would define this for me?

A. It's a command. *I almost use that tone with my children.* . . . Why, *just last night* he [her son John] was sitting here; I wasn't feeling well, and I said very nicely, "John, will you dry the dishes for me?" He said, "I'm tired." [In a brooding tone, again tense and clipped.] Then I said, "All right, John, when you're sick I take care of you and now I'm sick you don't have to do it." [Triumphantly] He got up and did the dishes. . . . Maybe that's what Kate Smith does, *she works on your conscience.* . . . *You stop to think, do I realize* . . . you see what I mean?

We have had repeated occasion to note that each type of interview question has major and subsidiary uses and that they are all designed to illuminate differing facets of what is, after all, the same concrete experience. In this case, the paralleling of experience helped *A* to clarify, after several earlier failures, the nature of her response to Smith's appeals for war bonds, rather than to bring out the personal context of that response. But as we have also noted, once the character of the response has been elaborated, the interviewer is well on the way to discovering its personal context.

An advantage of drawing upon parallel experiences is that personal contexts are ordinarily isolated in one step rather than by roundabout procedures. The interviewer must balance this advantage against possible disadvantages. He must decide whether it is preferable to ascertain the personal context quickly at the calculated risk of not uncovering it at all. The decision rests on his appraisal of the rapport established in the interview, on his intuitive guess as to the nature of the experience associated with the response, and on his judgment of the saliency of that experience. But general maxims cannot greatly help the interviewer to decide when a direct question of this kind is permissible, or even preferred; he must, in the end, base his decision on an appraisal, in the light of these considerations, of each specific case.

SUMMARY

The criterion of personal context is met by ascertaining the experiences and statuses which help account for definitions of a situation. This requires information about the experiential bases of responses and the contexts which imbue these responses with their distinctive meaning.

Procedures which have proved helpful in arriving at personal contexts include (1) the searching out of *identifications* of the interviewee with others in the situation, (2) the conversion of *projective statements* into personal reports, and (3) the drawing upon *experiences* of the interviewee which parallel those occurring in the situation under review. The first two are indirect procedures which minimize resistance to reports of private matters; the third is more nearly direct and might best be limited to interviews where there is solid rapport.

In his search for personal contexts, the interviewer may find himself allowing the focused interview to become diffuse. Often he has no guide to the pertinent experiences of the interviewee and, consequently, has little basis for deciding which direction this phase of the interview might best take. Under these conditions, the interview can move far afield, forgetful of the situation initially under review, and become a general conversation about matters suggested by the personal experiences which have been brought to light. This may serve other purposes, but not those of the focused interview. The interviewer should remember that, in a focused interview, the interest is in those matters which are, or can be, related to the stimulus situation. Interest in discovering personal contexts should not be permitted to result in prolonged digressions; these should be brought back in focus by relating the interviewee's prior experiences, dispositions and status to his definition of the particular situation.

CHAPTER VII

{ The Group Interview

As is evident from the materials cited in preceding chapters, the focused interview can be conducted with a *group* of people, rather than being necessarily confined to one individual at a time. There are advantages and disadvantages to the group interview, and these will be examined at some length in this chapter. On balance, it appears that the advantages of the focused interview of groups more than offset its disadvantages when one seeks clues to diverse definitions of the situation by a numerous body of individuals. This is not to say, of course, that an interview with ten people will yield ten times the amount of relevant data as the same kind of interview with a single individual. But ordinarily, it will yield a more diversified array of responses and afford a more extended basis both for designing systematic research on the situation in hand and for suggesting interpretations, grounded in experience, of experimental data on the effects of that situation.

Little enough is yet firmly known about the systematic differences between the types of data provided by interviews with individuals and with groups.[1] It is not at all certain

---

1. See, for example, E. S. Bogardus, "The group interview," *Journal of Applied Sociology,* 10 (1926) , 372 ff.; V. Edmiston, "The group interview," *Journal of Educational Research,* 37 (1944) , 593 ff.; J. D. Thompson and N. J. Demerath, "Some experiences with the group interview," *Social Forces,* 31 (1952) , 148 ff.

that the private interview is uniformly preferable to the interview with groups. It may even develop, on further study of this problem, that the group interview is preferable to the individual interview for certain types of problems. It is not the purpose of this chapter, however, to assess the comparative value of group and individual interviews. Instead, we propose to examine the major problems and procedures of group interviewing in general, problems arising from its *group* aspect rather than from its *focused* aspect. Whenever the general problems of interviewing groups are characteristically modified or intensified in the focused interview, these will be given special consideration.

The Setting of the Group Interview

SIZE OF GROUP

At least since the writings of Georg Simmel, sociologists have observed that even seemingly slight variations in the size of a face-to-face group will significantly affect the patterns of social interaction. In recent years, this insight has been more methodically developed, in research concerned with the bearing of the size of groups upon the roles adopted by its several members and, as in the case of conference groups, upon the character of the ensuing interaction.[2] As experimental research of this kind accumulates and results in attested findings, it will in due course provide a better-grounded basis for deciding upon the optimal sizes of groups for various kinds of interviews. The suggestions we make here are not based on the repeatedly confirmed findings of experiment but, just as the rest of this manual, represents the

---

2. See, for examples, Robert F. Bales and Edgar F. Borgotta, "Size of the group as a factor in the interaction profile," in Paul Hare, E. F. Borgatta and R. F. Bales, *Small Groups: Studies in Social Interaction* (New York: A. A. Knopf, 1955), pp. 396-413; John James, "A preliminary study of the size determinants in small group interaction," *American Sociological Review*, 16 (1951), 474-77.

best judgment we could reach from more than a decade of clinical experience with the focused interviewing of groups.

The size of the group should manifestly be governed by two considerations. It should not be so large as to be unwieldy or to preclude adequate participation by most members nor should it be so small that it fails to provide substantially greater coverage than that of an interview with one individual. Experience suggests that these twin purposes are best achieved in an interview group of some ten to twelve persons. Under certain conditions, it has been found possible to enlarge this number somewhat—to as many as fifteen to twenty—without undue deterioration in the value of the interview data and with some gain in its extensiveness. If, for example, the total sample of prospective interviewees is large enough or homogeneous enough to make it possible for each interview group to be made up of persons with similar social background and of the same degree of intelligence and education, the size of the group can be enlarged without sacrificing contributions from all its members. (The next section, dealing with the composition of the interview group, considers further the matter of homogeneity or heterogeneity of the group.) In those cases, also, where the interviewer is chiefly interested in the *range* of definitions of the situation, rather than in intensive reports of depth responses, the larger group is indicated. But, whatever the purpose, the group should not be enlarged to the point where the many constitute little more than an audience for the few who have opportunity to speak their mind.

COMPOSITION OF GROUP

It appears that the more socially and intellectually homogeneous the interview group, the more productive its reports. Correlatively, when the members of the group are of widely disparate social status or differ greatly in intelligence and educational attainments, the interview tends to be doubly damaged. Interviewees of widely differing social status often make comments or refer to experiences which are alien or meaningless to the rest. Although this diversity may interest the interviewer, it has uneven effects upon the others in the group. Some continue to be interested in what is being said, but others become restless and ultimately withdraw their attention. Interviewees of lower social status are particularly apt to feel inhibited as they hear those of higher status describe their responses. Subsequent personal interviews with lower-status members of the interview group have found that they tend to compare the relatively articulate and clearly formulated remarks of the others with what they would have said and avoid the invidious contrast by keeping their silence. Such heterogeneity leads those who feel themselves less capable of precise verbal expression to redefine the interview situation as a test of verbal facility. This comes to a head when interviewees in the group differ widely in extent of formal education.

The degree of homogeneity attainable in interview groups is of course dependent upon the size and nature of the sample from which they are drawn. When the sample is large enough, it is advisable to match the members of each interview group in several respects: education, occupation, and age being among the most pertinent for the run of studies. Often, however, the total sample will not be large enough to allow for homogeneity of interview groups in more than one or two respects, and it becomes necessary to decide which kind of homogeneity is preferable.

On the basis of experience to date, it seems that, for the purposes of most studies, *educational homogeneity* outranks all other kinds in making for effective interviews with groups.[3] Other differences, such as occupation, religion or even age may reduce the extent of common ground in the group and may lead to the difficulties we have indicated. But

---

3. Cf. also the observations in Hovland, Lumsdaine and Sheffield, *Experiments on Mass Communication*, p. 84.

when there is a wide spread in the education of interviewees, these difficulties are greatly compounded. Facility and ease of expression is the unspoken, but nevertheless controlling, criterion of "status" in these temporary interview groups since their members tend to appraise themselves and others by the criterion of the one activity which is the occasion for the group. As we have remarked, the less-educated, who are usually, though not inevitably, less facile of speech, tend to lapse into silence. Their silence, in turn, leads the interviewer to devote himself to the task of "drawing them out." The spontaneity of report, essential to the interview, dwindles and is replaced by reluctant and labored answers to questions. Not infrequently, the initially articulate members of the group take on the role of listeners to the exchange between the interviewer and the less articulate members. In the end, one of the chief advantages of the group interview— the interaction between members which activates otherwise forgotten recollections of experience—is wholly dissipated.

For these reasons, it seems advisable to arrange for a reasonable degree of educational homogeneity of the interview group even at the cost of having smaller groups than might otherwise be possible.

SPATIAL ARRANGEMENTS

There is reason to believe that the spatial distribution of an interview group appreciably affects the spontaneity and character of the reports. A circular pattern in which the interviewer is symbolically placed as one of the group has been found most conducive to full and spontaneous reporting; if the room does not lend itself to such an arrangement, a semicircle may be used instead. In no event should interviewees sit in rows facing the interviewer—an arrangement which is all too reminiscent of the schoolroom, with its associations of "correct" and "incorrect" answers to the school teacher's questions.

Nothing will countersay the social fact that the interviewer has a special role in the group. But if he is seated with the others, he becomes less the authoritative originating source of discussion. The circular arrangement promotes the informality and group interaction which is a prerequisite for an effective group interview.

The technical problem of recording the substance of the group interview is not considered in any detail here. Electronic devices with multiple microphones are available for recording the remarks of groups of this size. These have the limitations, however, of not identifying the speaker, a prime requisite for later analysis of the interview data. These devices can be effectively used in conjunction with an observer who records the sequence in which interviewees take part in the discussion. (The alternative practice of having each person identify himself before speaking is not recommended, for it interferes with the unself-conscious give-and-take between interviewees which ordinarily develops in the group interview.)

If a stenotypist, or expert stenographer is used, he should be inconspicuously placed on the margin of the group. The chairs of interviewees should be numbered to enable him to attribute comments to the person who has made them. (As we have intimated, this is essential if the responses of each individual are to be later collated for analysis.) Experience uniformly shows that an unobtrusively placed stenographer does not appreciably inhibit the free flow of report, particularly after the group interview has gained some momentum. Interviewees often remark, after the close of the interview, that they had scarcely noted the presence of the stenographer. The use of a stenographer provides an accurate transcript of the discussion, and leaves the interviewer free to concentrate on the interview rather than diverting his attention to the taking of necessarily incomplete notes.

Advantages of the Group Interview

The fact that a group interview secures data from several people rather than from one person is not its only, perhaps not even its principal, characterization. Social processes at work in a group make a group interview in some ways more productive, in others less productive, than an individual interview.

Even temporary groups soon evolve patterned roles characteristic of each of their members, as recent research has shown. Some become identifiable as initiators, advancing reports which touch upon matters not previously considered, others as regulators, helping to maintain the flow of conversation, and so on through a diversity of identifiable roles.[4]

Although each distinct characteristic of interaction in the group may operate either as advantage or as disadvantage, it is more serviceable here to consider these advantages or disadvantages in the large rather than attempt to single out their distinctive sources.

RELEASE OF INHIBITIONS

That social interaction in face-to-face groups commonly serves to evolve standards of behavior (which may be at odds with the previous behavior patterns of its members) is an empirical uniformity attested by much experience and one which is drawn upon by the most varied kinds of special-purpose groups. Under certain conditions these standards generated by group interaction will call for full and open reports of intimate experiences and sentiments (as is exemplified by sessions of Buchmanite groups and of Alcoholics Anonymous). The group interview utilizes the same kinds of social mechanism for releasing the inhibitions of indi-

---

4. For analyses of role differentiation in experimental groups which are pertinent to interview groups, see, for example, Hare, Borgotta and Bales, *op. cit.*

viduals who are otherwise reluctant to disclose what are for them intimately private matters.[5]

The major mechanism operating to this end, and the only one which need concern us here, is set in motion by the uneven distribution of such inhibitions among members of the group. Even in socially homogeneous groups numbering as many as ten or twelve members, it is likely that one or more will be considerably less inhibited than the rest. Since these are more willing than the others to speak of personal experiences and responses, they tend to be among the first to take active part in the discussion. As one ventilates his experiences, this encourages others to ventilate theirs. If, in turn, the reports of these self-starting interviewees are met with rewarding expressions of approval and support by the interviewer, they tend to establish a standard of conduct for the other, initially more inhibited, interviewees. The social process tends to be in this one direction for an obvious and important reason: the speech behavior of the less inhibited is at once put in evidence and can thereby provide an example for the rest of the group. The initial silence of the more inhibited, on the other hand, is not so directly conspicuous. Moreover, as we have suggested, the interviewer can also help tip the scales in favor of the evolving group pattern of free and uninhibited reports by manifesting his own approval, particularly in the early stages of the interview, of relatively uninhibited comments. Once this process is well under way, it tends to become self-maintaining and self-reinforcing.

Here is a run-of-the-mill example which, short and terse as it is, may be enough to serve as illustration. The interview

---

5. There are plentiful examples of how the group situation serves to release the inhibitions of some interviewees and to inhibit the responses of others. However, considerably more study along these lines is indicated. Experiments with matched samples, the persons in one set of samples being interviewed first individually and then in groups, with the sequence reversed for the second set, would throw considerable light on the problem.

group consists of Army inductees in basic training; they happen to be men of little education, ordinarily averse to the interview situation.

Int. What about crawling through the mud. . . . Here is a shot of that scene. What was interesting about that?

A. I liked the part that made the men keep clear, if they wanted to stay up. Seems as though they went along at one height as they were supposed to.

Int. What kind of impression did you have?

A. It was interesting all the way through on that.

B. I thought too, that it takes a lot of courage; takes a guy with guts to stay down there.

C. I have a brother who is in the infantry, and I was wondering whether he was under that too. He writes to me sometimes about it.

D. *I was kind of wondering if we could do the same thing as these boys do.*

A. *Me too.*

E. *Makes you feel like you can do it yourself.*

A isolates a part of the stimulus situation and goes on to make the bland comment that he found it "interesting." *B*, who had consistently taken a more active part in the interview, begins to give a more personal response and apparently encourages *C* to report a personal context of his response. By this point, *D* is ready to report that he has been led to self-appraisal by the scenes in the film—a considerable step beyond *A*'s initially impersonal characterization of the scene as "interesting." *A* now echoes *D*'s response and others begin to advance their own distinctive responses to the situation.

The evidence provided by numerous group interviews suggests that this can be a fairly general pattern; as each person in turn introduces a personal comment, he implicitly establishes a standard for the rest who progressively report more personalized responses, with the result that the discussion tends to flow in one direction: toward a successive release of inhibitions.

Something more should be said about the role of the

interviewer in promoting this process of lessened inhibition in the group interview. The first requirement is, of course, that he be alerted to the character of the process itself, so that he does not inadvertently fail to notice it at all. Following each "breakthrough" to a deeper and more personal report, he can facilitate progressively less inhibited reports, by expressing his own interest in what is being said. It is our experience that even a slight indication of this kind by the interviewer—"That's interesting—you say that it had you worried?"—serves to reinforce the process. Under no conditions, obviously, should the expressive interviewee be led to feel embarrassed, to feel that he has exposed his innermost feelings to the judgment of others. This would not only inhibit him from further reports of this kind, but would build a wall of reserve for the others. Encouragements of such reports, on the other hand, help set a group standard along the lines we have indicated, and, in due course, the interview proceeds on this level of uninhibited reporting with relatively little need for direction on the part of the interviewer.

All this seems evident enough. Yet there are occasions on which the interviewer inadvertently gives the impression that highly personal reports have been out of place. The interviewer may not take due notice of an interviewee's self-revelatory report and abruptly shift the level of the discussion to more objective matters, giving the interviewee as well as other members of the group the impression that such personal reports are unwanted or unfitting. Or the other extreme of overt behavior by the interviewer may lead to the same inhibiting result: he may seem too avidly interested in personal feelings as he prematurely pries into private matters. This excessive display of interest gives the interviewee (and the others) the impression that he has given too much of himself, that his feelings are being "indecently exposed." The most effective behavior by the interviewer is that which exhibits continued interest in such responses without running far ahead of the level reached by the interviewee. Brief remarks such as this—"That's an interesting point. Did any of the rest of you experience anything like that?"—will ordinarily serve the purpose. The interviewer remains *alert* to intimate reports which stimulate further self-revelations by others and he does not shut the door on them by changing the subject or by shifting the emphasis to another level. Above all, he does not give the impression that he is being unduly inquisitive about interviewees' private affairs or opinions.

WIDENING RANGE OF RESPONSE

A further, almost self-evident, advantage of the group interview accrues from the occasion it affords for interviewing a number of people instead of a single person. The more people reporting, the greater the ascertained range of variation in pertinent opinions and responses. Particularly in a *focused* group interview, this means that the interviewer discovers a wide variety of definitions of the objectively identical situation. In the following short excerpt from a group interview, for example, a single question elicits varied reports from five members of the group.

> *Int.* Was there anything in the film that gave you the impression that the German people were backing up Hitler or not?
>
> *A.* Yes.
>
> *B.* Yes.
>
> *Int.* What?
>
> *A.* They were cheering Hitler and Goering, they praised him and things like that.
>
> *C.* They weren't civilians, they were army men.
>
> *D.* If a man stood behind you with a tommy gun and told you to cheer, you would cheer too.
>
> *A.* Who makes up the German government? It's the soldiers. The only thing left is men who are so old they can't walk. . . .

    B.   When Hitler came in they didn't have a majority.

    E.   Just so long as the German people regret what has gone before, there is no reason to think they are responsible for them.

The scope provided by the group interview makes it especially useful as a preliminary step to developing a questionnaire or response schedule to be administered to a large sample, for it elicits a greater variety of otherwise unanticipated responses than an individual interview and thus affords a basis for ensuring a more adequate coverage of responses in the questionnaire.

ACTIVATING FORGOTTEN DETAILS

The interaction in the group may not only lessen inhibition of intimate reporting; it may also serve to bring to each individual's mind details of his experience which would otherwise not be recalled.

As various pertinent matters are brought out in the group interview, it is probable that each interviewee will have matters brought to his attention which he would have overlooked or forgotten had he been privately interviewed. To be sure, the interviewer can serve this same function of activating memory in the private interview. But if he, in his distinctive status, adopts this role of directing the attention of the interviewee, he may inadvertently assign importance to the selected subjects which they did not in fact have. The interaction between interviewees is, or can be, of a substantially less controlling kind.

Toward this end, it is essential that the interviewer help develop, at the very outset of the group interview, a group atmosphere in which there are no "correct" or "incorrect" answers, but only self-exploratory reports of personal response. He can indicate as a matter of course that responses will doubtlessly vary in some cases and not in others. Once the members of the groups come to recognize that diversity of response is not exceptional, they will feel free to report their distinctive reactions without feeling that they are "disagreeing" with their fellow-interviewees. Thus, when one person alludes to an element in the situation temporarily forgotten by another, the latter may well be stimulated to report *his* response to the reinstated part of the situation.

This process is not, of course, an unmixed blessing, as we shall shortly see.[6] It is obviously a liability in interviews designed, among other things, to ascertain the extent of recall by each individual. But for many other purposes, this feature of the group interview serves an activating function not readily duplicated in the private interview.

Disadvantages of the Group Interview

There are, then, certain advantages in the interviewing of groups as compared with the interviewing of individuals. As suggested earlier, these advantages are somewhat offset by corresponding disadvantages. These will be pointed out briefly here, and the next section of this chapter will consider how these disadvantages may be minimized, or even converted into assets.

RESPONSES TO INTERVIEW SITUATION

In examining the consequences of social interaction in the interview group, we have thus far looked primarily to its functions. But, manifestly, such interaction can also be dysfunctional for the process and purposes of the interview. Controversies or amicable discussion may spring up among interviewees and their subsequent reports may be more nearly related to this interplay of personalities and status claims in the group than to the subject matter on which the interview is centered. As one among many cases in point,

6. For a compact summary of research on the ways in which individual behavior is modified in a face-to-face group, see H. H. Kelley and J. W. Thibaut, "Experimental studies of group problem solving and process," in Gardner Lindzey, (ed.) ., *Handbook of Social Psychology* (Cambridge, Mass.: Addison-Wesley Publishing Company, 1954) , II, pp. 735-785.

consider this example of the sentiments expressed by one interviewee working upon the sentiments of another.

> *A.* The impression that mob scene gave me, if it happened in a little town further south, a colored boy down there would commit murder and one man will yell "Let's hang him" and pretty soon the whole town is out. . . .
>
> *B.* I would like to go into that point a little. I am from the South.

Here, obviously, the Southerner *B* has temporarily lost sight of the subject under review, as he responds to the violation of his sentiments by *A*. In a private interview, *A*'s allusion to a lynching mob would presumably not have evoked a defensive outburst by the interviewer, whatever his cultural provenience. In the group interview, the remark threatens to stir up a storm of conflicting sentiments, none of which is pertinent to the situation on which the interview is focused. The interviewer adopts a nonpartisan but firm position and promptly redirects the attention of the group to a more pertinent matter, but this is at best an expedient designed to control a situation that would not have arisen at all in the private interview.

> *Int.* We don't want to fight the Civil War here. Let me ask you another question. . . .

This problem of irrelevancies generated by interaction among members of the group is particularly acute in the focused interview which aims to search out responses to a designated stimulus situation rather than the enduring sentiments and opinions of interviewees. It is not enough that the interviewer serve as a moderator regulating the tensions developed in the group. He must help the group maintain its focus on the pertinent situation and, without acting the disciplinarian, redirect their attention to that situation.

The "leader effect." Wherever groups of people gather to talk, some are more articulate than others. This may be the result of fewer inhibitions, general volubility, higher intelligence, higher social status or greater familiarity with the topic under discussion. We have considered the functions of such variability in releasing the inhibitions of certain members of the group; it remains now to consider some of its dysfunctions. For whatever the basis of this variability,[7] it is possible that the more articulate members will, deliberately or without intent, adopt and be accorded the role of a leader in the interview group. A few such leader effects require notice at this point.

1. Considerations of social status to one side for the moment, the person who expresses emphatic opinions or who documents his responses in great detail may influence reports by other members of the group. The less articulate often respond as though they had concluded, "Well, he seems to know what he is talking about—I guess I feel that way too." As his temporary status of leader becomes established, the others look to him for guidance and tend, consciously or otherwise, to report reactions similar to his or simply indicate agreement with him.

2. When several such candidates for leader turn up in an interview group, they may, between them, virtually monopolize the discussion. Others become listeners rather than participants, as though to say: "They seem to know it all; let them talk." The lively give-and-take between the few, whether competitive or co-operative, usurps the attention of the rest of the group.

3. In a focused group interview, the articulate person with a good memory may "structure" the stimulus situation for the others. At the extreme, the "followers" may report their responses only to what the "leader" brings into discussion rather than have this serve to supplement their self-remembered foci of attention.

---

7. T. Staton, "An analysis of the effects of individuals in seminar discussion," *American Psychologist,* 3 (1948), 267 (abstract).

INTERRUPTIONS OF CONTINUITY

Quite apart from the leader effect, an excessive multiplicity of topics may be advanced in the group interview with the result that no one of these is explored in substantial detail. When one interviewee introduces a matter wholly unrelated to the substance of the interview, this can and often does interrupt the continuity of group discussion. It is for the interviewer to be alerted to this bid for digression and, as in the following example (albeit not with notable deftness), to return the discussion to the matter in hand.

> [Interviewer asks what impression the documentary motion picture gave of Hitler.]
>
> *A.* He is not foolish, I'll tell you that.
> *B.* He is just a bully, in my estimation.
> *C.* He is a smart man and he knows how to handle his men and everything.
> *D.* *If this were a round table discussion, I would argue that point.*
> *Int.* In a sense it is, but on the other hand, we have a limited amount of time and my primary interest, after all, is finding out about the film. . . .
> *E.* One thing about the picture. . . .

Here the interview is flowing along smoothly with various interviewees beginning to assemble an inventory of diverse perceptions and responses. *D* interrupts by transferring the discussion from the level of response to the argumentative level of the merits of a response. The interviewer does what he can to restore the *status ante quo,* but the continuity of response has been broken and *E* turns to an entirely different matter.

A train of thoughtful or expressive responses by some is not infrequently brought to a halt by others in the interview group who unintentionally set up a kind of road block. Moreover, the interviewees who find difficulty in putting their responses into words will at times welcome such interruptions which release them from the obligations of reporting. As one interviewee gropes for adequate expression, another, more facile, interviewee may interrupt and "explain" what is being ineptly said or offer a comment of his own. The relatively inarticulate person may take the line of least resistance and gratefully subside into silence. Or again, if one interviewee is emotionally blocked when he reaches the point of touching on a deeply personal matter, before the interviewer can help him to go on with his report, another may interrupt. The interviewer who is alerted to these problems can, however, often aid the interviewees thus interrupted to take up where they had been forced to leave off.

INHIBITING EFFECT OF THE GROUP

As we have noted, the interview group may stimulate some of its members to open discussion and inhibit others.

Resistance to reporting "before" the group is of course most marked for matters which threaten to humiliate the speaker before his fellows. It is difficult enough to speak of socially disapproved feelings or behavior in a private session with a sympathetic interviewer who has made it abundantly clear that he does not pass judgment; the difficulty is compounded by the presence of others who often make it evident by their behavior that they do not reserve their judgment of the speaker. For these obvious reasons, interviewees may find it humiliating to "confess," in the quasi-public situation of the group interview, to certain attitudes, sentiments or experiences.

But this inhibiting effect of the group probably varies greatly according to the nature and aims of the interview as these are experienced by members of the group. In the focused interview, for example, the stage is set not so much for reports of personal and possibly damaging confidences, of enduring attitudes and feelings, as for reports of responses to a particular situation to which all members of the group have been exposed. The interview consequently tends to take the form of a conversation among people who have been involved in the same situation and are interested in comparing notes on their experience, and this operates to counteract the inhibitions which might obtain in the open exploration of wholly private and unshared experience. Nevertheless, there are indications that some interviewees hesitate to report responses when these are greatly different from those reported by others, in the belief that their perceptions or feelings "must be unsound" since they differ materially from those of the others.

An interviewee may not be less articulate in a group interview than in a private interview, but may be articulate about quite different matters. In the private interview, he may report more of himself, be readier to provide that information which enables the inquirer to reconstruct the personal context of his response; in the group interview, he may adapt to the presence of several others by largely confining himself to reports of his response, telling less of the contexts which help account for his more or less distinctive response. Here again, clinical experience serves to detect a problem which would lend itself to experimental study: comparisons of reports by persons alternately interviewed in private and in groups about responses to particular situations would serve to uncover differences in the level of reporting under the two sets of conditions.

On occasion, also, interviewees may define the situation of the group interview as one in which each member *should* take roughly equal part and in which none *should* dominate the discussion "at the expense" of others. Although such normative definitions of appropriate behavior in the group interview do not appear in the transcripts of the interview itself, there is evidence that they can enter in to reduce the participation of some in the discussion. As interviewees have occasionally put it after the close of an interview, they wanted "to give someone else a chance" or felt that they "had said enough already." To some extent, these group-evolved norms are useful in helping to ensure and to maintain participation by all members of the group. For, as we have seen in the section on "the leader effect," initially marked disproportions in participation can gradually result in a few individuals virtually monopolizing the conversation. However, when these operating norms of the group serve to inhibit reports by some who have a distinct contribution to make, equal participation by all becomes a self-contained standard which vitiates the objectives of the interview. It is sometimes far from evident that such inhibition is at work, but the experienced interviewer will often detect signs that one or another interviewee is curbing a remark he was about to make and will provide the occasion for these barely suppressed comments to be made after all.

Procedures

As has been implied in the foregoing review, the distinctive advantages and disadvantages of the group interview are to a considerable extent potentialities rather than fixed and inevitable certainties. They constitute tendencies toward one or another outcome, but the interviewer can appreciably affect the degree to which these tendencies become realized or remain unexpressed. This is only to say that *some* forms of social interaction will occur in the interview group and that it is the office of the interviewer to minimize the occurrence of those which militate against the purposes of the interview. Experience has shown that some measure of such control can be effectively and unobtrusively exercised without requiring the interviewer to adopt the role of one who is policing the discussion. It is the purpose of this section to examine procedures which serve to hold the potential disadvantages of the group interview in check and, at times, to convert them into definite assets.

FACILITATING REPORTS BY ENTIRE GROUP

For the purposes of the interview, those who do not take

part in the discussion are of course only nominally members
of the group. They neither provide accounts of experience
of the kind which could be aggregated from a series of single-
person interviews nor interact significantly with others to
stimulate the kinds of reports which are elicited by the group
situation. In seeking to obtain data on responses from all
members of the group, the interviewer is confronted with a
threefold problem: first, to keep the most fluent members
of the group from dominating the interview, without curbing spontaneity or damaging rapport; second, to draw out
interviewees who at first say little or nothing; and third, to
obtain substantial coverage of the entire group in regard to
each pertinent subject matter.

1. *Controlling loquacious interviewees.* There are two
familiar types of situation in which the interviewer will want
to restrain an interviewee from further discussion of a particular point: when it is plainly a digression, which gives
no evidence of reverting to the subject matter under review,
and again, when he practically monopolizes the interview.
In either case, the interviewer can more effectively intervene
without arousing antagonism if, instead of having to improvise in each situation of this kind, he uses expedients
previously designed for the purpose.

This does not require a heavy insistence that only certain
matters be discussed. It does, however, require the interviewer to be thoroughly aware that a digression has occurred and to make it easy for the speaker to return to a
circumstantial account of his experience. When a member
of the group has digressed, the interviewer can pick up a
particular reference or allusion in the generally irrelevant
remarks and relate it to a subject matter to be considered
in the interview, thus redirecting the discussion. (For example, "You mentioned a number of factors that were important in the defence of Russia. . . .") Properly done, this
is not so much an interruption by the interviewer which,

particularly in the presence of others, might puncture the self-esteem of the interviewee as it is a manifestation of interest in what is being said. Except for those interviewees who are obsessively preoccupied with a particular subject, redirection of this sort is generally experienced neither as an affront nor as a calculated change of subject, for they have often held conversations which hang together only loosely, as one speaker responds to the remarks of the other with a new topic.

When a loquacious interviewee has been holding forth at some length, so that others have been unable to express their opinions, the interviewer can adopt a slight variation of the procedure designed to direct the discussion toward other members of the group without violating the ego feelings of the talkative one. In the example that follows, it will be noticed that the interviewer invites wider participation while making it clear that he hopes to hear later from the interviewee who has been encroaching unduly upon the limited time available for the interview. The interviewer's request for more widely dispersed reports is in accord with the con-sensus ordinarily evolving in the group which calls for participation by most or all members, and the social import of the request is further cushioned by the proposal to return to the original speaker.

Int. Why do you think the Russians made that pact?
A. [Discusses his ideas at length.]
Int. Do any of the rest of you have different ideas?
A. [Continues his account.]
    [Several other interviewees say a few words.]
A. I think. . . .
Int. Let's get the ideas from some of the others for a minute and come back to you. What did you think was the reason, *B*?
B. I don't know.

The interviewer effectively checks *A* who has been dominating the discussion for some time. But instead of redirecting the question to the group as a whole so that those for whom the matter has some salience will respond, the interviewer prematurely puts the question to one member of the group in particular. As it happens, *B* has nothing to say on the subject and what might have been a well-designed detour becomes a temporary impasse. This episode leads us directly to consideration of a second problem of obtaining adequate participation by the group.

2. *Activating reticent interviewees.* It happened that in the preceding case, *B* had been silent for a considerable time. The interviewer evidently aimed to accomplish two things at once: to restrain *A* and to draw *B* back into the discussion. But *B* has given no indication that this particular subject has held any interest for him or that he has ever given the matter any thought. He appears to be brought up short by the direct question, which he ostensibly answers. He "doesn't know" why the Russians entered into the pact and his laconic reply puts an abrupt end to the matter.

Episodes such as this one provide the basis for the rule that generally uncommunicative interviewees in the group interview should not have questions put directly to them unless they have previously given evidence of definite interest in the matter. In this one case, the interviewer neglected the rule and was met with a disclaimer of knowledge or opinion. In other comparable cases, the reticent interviewee thus singled out for special attention will, in his embarrassment and confusion, shrink even further into his shell. Or the direct question will evoke a hardly disguised expression of hostility:

Int. What were *you* going to say, *E*?
E. I wasn't going to say anything.

In our judgment, the one occasion on which it may be effective to address a question directly to a generally reticent interviewee who at the time shows no signs of readiness to speak is when a new subject is being introduced for discussion. Even in such instances, however, it appears advisable to have the question open-ended and unstructured: "What were your feelings about that, *B*?" or "What impressed you about that part, *C*?" The focus upon the stimulus situation to which he has been exposed and the request for a report of experience on a matter which has not yet been reviewed at length by more fluent members of the group afford a maximum scope for reply by the reticent interviewee.

The group interview requires the interviewer to be observant of behavioral and verbal cues of readiness to take part in the discussion, and particularly so, to cues provided by those interviewees who have proved to be generally uncommunicative. When they are on occasion poised to speak up, only to retreat as more voluble persons take the lead, the interviewer can indicate by an appropriate gesture that he is interested in hearing from them. Marked interest in what they have said may provide further incentives for them to take the initiative later in the interview.

3. *Extending coverage of group.* The suggested expedients for controlling excessively voluble interviewees and for stimulating reticent ones are designed to make for wider discussion of matters under review than would otherwise occur. Supplementing these special procedures is the general practice of arranging for a pattern in which many if not all members of the group report spontaneously on each subject considered in the interview. To promote this objective, the interviewer will find it useful to adopt the practice, with some regularity, of remaining silent after each new question until it is clear that all interviewees who have something to say in reply have done so, and only then to reinstate the same question for the other members of the group, along lines such as these:

> How about the rest of you on that?
>
> Did any of you get some other ideas?
>
> Would all of you agree on that, or would some of you disagree?

Did it give any of you some different impressions?

When these two steps still fail to elicit comments from some in the group, it often proves useful to rephrase the question slightly with the object of striking a responsive note among those hitherto silent.

> [Interviewer asks what the U. S. should do if the German people were to overthrow Hitler, put someone else in his place, and offer peace terms.]
>
> *A.* I think maybe that would be all right . . . if we could police them.
> *B.* I think that would be all right if they would let us disarm them.
> *C.* I think it wouldn't be right . . . it would come out again sooner or later.
> *Int.* Are there any other ideas on that?
> *D.* I agree with him that Goering or someone else would be just as bad as Hitler . . . we would have another war.
> *E.* I think we should go ahead and disarm them and leave enough men over there to patrol the country.
> *Int.* Let's put it this way. Suppose the Germans offered the U. S. a separate peace so we wouldn't have to send any more men over there. What do you think we ought to do?
> *F.* Well, if we made a separate peace, I think it would be wrong. . . .

In this interview group of ten, spontaneous comments are made by three; the extensive question elicits comments from two others; and the reworded version leads to an observation by yet another. These brief remarks can now become the basis for more intensive probes. As this practice is repeated in the group interview, the pattern of various members responding spontaneously to the same question becomes increasingly established, with progressively less need for having all three types of questions in each introduction to a new subject.

DEAD SILENCE AND PREGNANT SILENCE

The contingency perhaps most dreaded by the novice interviewer is that of being faced by utter silence after he has asked a question or introduced a new subject. The same seeming predicament may of course occur in a one-person interview, but in this less complex situation, even the inexperienced interviewer finds it a less threatening problem with which he can somehow cope. But in the group interview, he often takes silence to mean that he has made a false step, that he has prematurely pushed into a sensitive area or phrased his question ineptly. In effect, he tends to assume that the silence of the entire group registers invidious judgment of his behavior. He is beset by social anxiety.

Yet much of this anxiety is misplaced. Not all silences are ominous. Particularly when a group consensus has evolved in the course of the interview, the occasional moment of silence may be only a prelude to spontaneous and full-fashioned reports of sentiments or experiences, the silence having been occasioned by the effort to sort out the varied responses brought to mind by the question. Or the silence may indeed signal that the question has touched upon matters imbued with affect, some of which will in due course find expression. There is, in short, the pregnant silence, as experienced interviewers well know.

In fact, unless the interview has taken a course in which the group is charged with hostility toward the interviewer, such periodic silences are usually productive. If the interviewer remains relaxed, and says nothing for a moment or two, one or another member of the group will ordinarily break the silence. This requires the interviewer to have some degree of self-assurance and to feel relatively secure that he has identified the occasion for what it is. But if he is, instead, anxious to evoke some response—almost any response—he will commonly break out with a rash of questions in the desperate hope that at least one of these will elicit a reply.[8] His efforts are not unlike those of the child who, having

---

8. See also the passing notice taken of this pattern of behavior in the section on mutational questions.

planted a seed, digs it up at short intervals to see how much it has grown—and they are typically just as productive. Consider the following examples taken from our dustbin of conspicuous errors:

> How did you like the combination of these various types of music in one program? Was the selection of numbers a wise one? Did it interest you? Would it make you listen to it if you were home?
>
> How do you really feel when you see scenes of that sort? Does it interest you at all? Would you rather not see it?

Engulfed in this deluge of questions and discouraged by the apparent expectation that they answer all of them, interviewees ordinarily succeed in answering none. The flurry of queries tends to dispel the social atmosphere conducive to the effective group interview, as the interviewer is cast in the role of an inquisitor, charged with anxiety and uninterested in the group, except as a source of needed data. Confronted with a multiplicity of questions, the group is quick to sense the insecurity and discomfort of the interviewer. Altogether, few things can be more paralyzing in an interview than a long, unbroken series of questions.

When it is periodically introduced during intervals of silence, the pattern of a chain of questions will sometimes spread into other phases of the interview, as is the case in the following short passage.

> *Int.* You remember there was a scene showing gangsters in a car?
> *A.* Dillinger.
> *Int.* Yes. Do you remember that? What in the world was that all about? What was it intended to bring out?

Having ascertained that the interviewee had identified the scene in question, a relaxed interviewer would simply have encouraged him to report his response to it, possibly by some version of his final question: "What did that bring out?" But this interviewer manifests his anxiety by exaggerated phrasing of one question ("What in the world was that all about?") and by reiteration of substantially the same content in a rapid-fire series of three questions. *A* does not respond at all and another interviewee intervenes with a general comment which leads to a new subject, as the scene which the interviewer wished to bring into focus is entirely lost to view.

There is, then, no more necessity in the group interview than in other conversational groups for immediately breaking into the occasional silence. Should it extend for some time, the interviewer can ordinarily preclude the rise of group tension by putting his question in slightly modified form. In the comparatively rare event that this too elicits no response, he simply registers the fact that the matter in point is evidently of no consequence—"You found that this didn't impress you at all?"—and turns to another topic. The essential requirement is to recognize in advance that situations of this kind occasionally develop in the group interview and that it is possible to cope with them by the use of premeditated expedients in those cases in which the group itself does not break the silence. Advance recognition of this will do much to curb the anxiety of the interviewer with its attendant loss of control over the situation.

REGULATING GROUP INTERACTION

As we noted in previous sections of this chapter, social interaction among members of the group can promote or thwart the purposes of the interview. As he observes the course of give-and-take among them, the interviewer can usually assess the character of the process. In the following case, for example, he intervenes to encourage the expression of diverse opinions through an exchange among interviewees.

> *Int.* Well, do you think we ought to do anything like that [bomb civilian areas]?
> *A.* No.
> *B.* If we would, I wouldn't fight.
> *Int.* How about some of the rest of you? As I said before, I don't expect all of you to agree. . . .

> *C.* I think we should give them the same medicine they are giving us.
>
> *A.* That isn't what we are fighting for . . . we are trying to create a better way.

At the outset, *A* registers his opinion on the matter at issue by an unelaborated negative. The interviewer infers from what has been said on related matters earlier in the interview that the group is not of one opinion on this and that *A*'s remark stems from still unreported sentiments. Thereupon, he encourages an interchange of views among interviewees, with the apparent result that *A* is stimulated by the opposed views of *C* to elaborate his own sentiments.

In contrast, the following excerpt exemplifies cumulative interaction between members of the group which leads far afield from the subject in hand.

> *Int.* Do you think seeing a picture like that would make anyone mad at the German people as well as the leaders?
>
> *Group* [Expresses general agreement.]
>
> *Int.* Do you think it is a good idea or not?
>
> *A.* No, I don't think so because the people are not to blame for what the soldiers do.
>
> *B.* You have to kill the people.
>
> *C.* Soldiers are backed by the people . . . so it is partly the people's fault.
>
> *D.* No, it isn't.
>
> *A.* No, I disagree with you, because any time you control the military you control the nation.
>
> *B.* I betcha any money you could catch a lot of those Germans and a lot don't want to fight.
>
> *A.* But they do.
>
> *Int.* Did you get the impression from the film, let's say, that the Nazi soldiers in action don't want to fight?

To the point at which *A* remarks that he disagrees with *D*, the exchange of opinions among interviewees is pertinent to the subject under review. The comments that follow not only depart from this subject, but the expressed differences of opinion begin to lead to defensive re-affirmations of views.

The interviewer promptly intercedes at this point, without allying himself to any of these extraneous views, and redirects attention to the stimulus situation by picking up *B*'s statement and relating it to the film.

The interviewer may, of course, err in his running appraisal of the direct consequences for the interview of social interaction in the group. There are all shades of variation in the character of this interaction which fail to be adequately distinguished in the simple distinction between those which are functional and those which are dysfunctional for the interview. Nevertheless, the distinction can serve as a useful beginning to more discriminating appraisals of cases in process. When the interviewer finds that the interaction is cumulating into irrelevance or unproductive conflict, he can redirect the discussion, without passing invidious judgment on those who have taken part in it. Even a comparatively clumsy effort, such as that of the interviewer in the following passage, can serve the purpose.

[The interview has been dealing with Nazi plans to overrun other nations.]

A. I don't think the point was brought out that there was German rule outside of Germany.

B. No, it didn't bring that out.

C. If I remember right, I came into the army of my own free will, to protect my wife and three children so that they wouldn't be bombed right here in this country.

D. If I remember right, I came from a special invitation.

Int. I don't think I had better start getting into your histories to find out why you got into the war. . . .

Although the interviewer does not directly discredit *D*'s facetious remark, he does imply that the discussion has turned to matters irrelevant to the interview. His purpose of directing the discussion into other channels would have been better served had he foregone the implied judgment and related the antecedent remarks of interviewees to the film under review. Nevertheless, he has identified the beginnings of a group-induced digression and intervened before it has drifted even farther afield.

We have observed that not infrequently, one interviewee will interrupt another in the group, before he can manage to give the substance of what he has begun to say. In some cases, barely a word is allowed to pass before the other tries to anticipate what would have been said:

> *Int.* What gives you that impression?
> *A.* Because. . . .
> *B.* They were training for years.

In other cases, he will interrupt to pursue his own line of thought:

> *C.* They have to fight or die, but down in their own hearts. . . .
> *D.* Wouldn't it be better for them to fight and die or revolt and die and keep out of the war? Like this, they will be doing more good to mankind. The people themselves want to fight or they wouldn't be fighting like that.

In both types of instance, the interviewer may find himself inclined to put an end to the interruption and to have the discussion revert to the first interviewee who might thus continue to report what he had in mind. This practice exacts a price in interview rapport. It tends to discourage spontaneity of response for the interruption, however inconvenient, does ordinarily represent a direct expression of intense opinion or sentiment, uninhibited by the niceties of polite behavior. Bringing the interruption to an abrupt close and pointedly returning to the initial speaker may not only be experienced by the interruptor as a rebuke but, if often repeated, may restrain spontaneous participation by the rest of the group seeking to avoid a similar *faux pas.*

The interviewer need not adopt this authoritarian role. Once the interruption has occurred, it might well be permitted to run its course (unless, as we have noted, it develops into a lengthy digression). At times, the interrupted speaker will himself return at the first opportunity to what he had started to say. If he does not, the interviewer, having taken due note of his preceding comment, reverts to it at a later, more appropriate time or addresses a question, based on this comment, to the group at large. When there is a genuine sense of incompletion on the part of the previously interrupted speaker, he will probably take the occasion to reach closure.

ASCERTAINING RESPONSE FREQUENCIES

The relatively unstandardized group interview is scarcely an appropriate tool for obtaining systematic counts of the frequency of designated responses. Such enumerations require the use of questionnaires, standardized interviews with aggregates of individuals, and other comparable standardized techniques. In some instances, however, the interviewer will have a particular reason for wanting a rough estimate of the relative frequency of certain attitudes or other responses emerging in the group, or in an aggregate of interview groups. Attitudes may have become polarized; perceptions of a situation may be of two or three kinds; a presumed consensus is found to be fragmented. Since not all members of the group may have spoken to the matter at hand, the interviewer seeks a complete enumeration of unelaborated attitudes, perceptions or values. He states the alternatives and asks for a show of hands.

In any case, it appears advisable to keep such enumerations to a feasible bare minimum in each group interview. For at best, calling for a show of hands is a somewhat formal procedure, far removed from the informality of expressive conversation. The interviewer is conspicuously in command of the proceedings as interviewees are given their instructions. The change in group atmosphere is considerable, and it may take some time to re-establish the flow of discussion.

In the event that an enumeration is to be made, the interviewer should first make reasonably certain that the alternative responses have emerged with some clarity in the interview. He has then to formulate the essential content of these alternatives clearly in his own mind before he undertakes to present them in succinct and balanced form to the group. Neglect of both these desiderata in the following instance results in characteristic confusion.

> *Int.* That brings up a very interesting question. Supposing, say, next month, the German people were to get together and overthrow Hitler and throw out the Nazi party and then go back to their prewar boundaries, do you think we should accept that offer or do you think we should keep on fighting?
>
> Let's take a show of hands on that. Let me state the thing again. I want to get every man's opinion. Here is the thing. If the German people were to throw over Hitler and the Nazis were to make peace and go back to their prewar boundaries, how many of you think we ought to accept that kind of offer and try to make peace with them?

It will be agreed that the question, with its series of conditional clauses, is not a model of clarity. Hearing his own first formulation, the interviewer evidently recognizes that it is cumbrous and opaque. He hastily tries to redeem the fault, before having arrived at a clearer statement, and succeeds only in eliminating the balanced alternatives which constituted the sole merit of his preceding version.

Furthermore, it seems that the issue had not been joined in the preceding discussion. If it had, the interviewer might have more readily arrived at a short, clear statement of alternatives before asking for a show of hands.

In the contrasting case that follows, the interviewer has no difficulty in stating the balanced alternatives, which bear upon the film under discussion and which arise directly from the preceding remark by an interviewee.

> *Int.* What did the Russians do during the Polish campaign?

> *A.* They joined hands with Germany at that time, didn't they?
>
> *Int.* Oh, yes, the Russian-German pact. Now here is a point I am curious about. Before you saw that film, how many of you remembered about the German pact and how many of you had forgotten it? Those of you who had forgotten it, raise your hands.
> [Four raise their hands.]
>
> *Int.* And the rest of you remembered it. Well, do you think the Russians were justified in making that pact at that time or not?

That even this straightforward and far from complex procedure had best not be improvised anew in each case, but should rather be a uniform sequence in which the group interviewer has become practiced, is illustrated by the last remark in this passage. The interviewer has stated the balanced alternatives and has found that four members of the group assign themselves to one of these alternatives (that of having forgotten the designated fact). The next step would properly involve a comparable count of those in the other category (that of having remembered the fact). Instead, the interviewer makes the possibly mistaken assumption that the two categories are exhaustive: "And the rest of you remembered it." Explicit inquiry might well have found a third class of those who cannot say, with any confidence, whether they had remembered it or not. There is no less occasion for providing for a "don't know" response in these "oral questionnaires" than in written questionnaires.

When such counts are taken in the group, the polarization of responses of course becomes evident both to the interviewer and to the group at large. This affords a basis for interviewees to elaborate the meanings of their responses. Since, in this situation, interviewees often try to vindicate their views rather than to clarify them—especially when the responses express sentiments or attitudes—the interviewer needs to focus attention on the meanings of the responses and not on their justification.

It will be noted, also, that the count is taken soon after

the subject has been introduced and is only then followed by intensive discussion of the subject. For obvious reasons, it is necessary to reverse the sequence adopted in parliamentary practice where a vote is taken after the merits of proposed legislation have been debated. For in the interview, the object is to have the group situation serve primarily to facilitate the report rather than to shape its content. If full discussion were to precede the count, it would presumably affect the later summary of responses.

In general, then, formal enumerations of responses should be held to a minimum in the group interview which is not optimally suited to the purpose. When estimates of frequencies of response are needed, the interviewer will find it advisable to arrange (1) for counts to be made after the subject area has emerged in the interview, (2) to have the alternative responses clearly in mind before submitting them in succinct and balanced fashion to the group, (3) to have a show of hands on all the alternatives, thus allowing for the possibility that some interviewees are not able to report their responses at all, and (4) to have the formal enumeration followed by intensive discussion of the meanings of the responses.

COUNTERACTING THE LEADER EFFECT

Earlier in this chapter, we noted that some individuals typically emerge as informal leaders in the interview group, taking appreciably greater part in the discussion and, to some unknown degree, presumably influencing the reports of the others. We noted also that social homogeneity of the interview group does something to curb this development, but does not serve to prevent it. Although the interviewer does not eliminate the leader effect, he can keep it somewhat in check and can roughly assess the extent to which it has occurred in each group.

As the informal status structure of the interview group emerges, the interviewer can usually identify the individuals who tend to initiate discussions of new subjects or to take the lead in expressing their opinions. This identification of course is far from being precise, nor need it be. It is ordinarily possible for the interviewer to distinguish the more from the less active participants at each phase of the interview and to stimulate discussion by the less articulate, by means of procedures described in preceding chapters. He can make a special point of following out sketchy observations advanced by the less active members of the group, express particular interest in their comments and focus, for a time, on subjects with which they have indicated marked involvement. This helps individuals shift their roles as the interview proceeds. Even though this does not result in equalizing the degree and character of participation, it does serve to mitigate the leader effect to some extent.

Short questionnaires, designed to elicit a summary of attitudes and opinions bearing on the chief subjects of the interview, are often administered before the interview has begun.[9] Comparison of these data with the qualitative reports of the interview can provide some basis for appraising the extent of the leader effect. The more elaborate qualitative reports are coded in terms of the categories used in the questionnaire to determine the extent of change in expressed attitudes and opinions among those identified as leaders and as followers. Although such changes cannot be unequivocally assigned to social interaction in the interview—some may be the result of continued self-exploration which has also been taking place—greater change among followers than leaders is presumptive evidence of the leader effect. The analysis of various parts of the interview data can be accordingly qualified in the light of this evidence.

---

9. Cf. Hovland, Lumsdaine and Sheffield, *op. cit.*, pp. 84, 107.

CHAPTER VIII

} # Selected Problems

Preceding chapters have dealt with the major formal objectives of the focused interview and with procedures designed to help realize each of these. Other problems and
practices, having to do with the conduct of the interview
rather than bearing specifically upon one or another of these
objectives, have until now received only passing attention.
This concluding chapter examines several of these more general or pervasive problems.

Opening the Interview

As we have periodically noted, the social atmosphere of
the interview significantly affects the extent to which pertinent reports are elicited and the ease with which this is
accomplished. A tedious interview is usually a profitless one.
The interviewer can do much to establish the tone of the
interview by clarifying, at the outset, the purposes of the
inquiry and by defining his role as well as that of the interviewees. It is for him to set the stage so that the others will
have genuine interest in playing their parts.

EXPLANATION OF PURPOSE

However varied the specific purposes of focused interviews, they have in common the general purpose of trying
to discover the meanings of a designated situation for those

who have been exposed to it. Interviewees are being asked to provide data which can be analyzed to yield uniformities of human behavior or to provide bases for future action (to improve documentary films, to improve the architectural design of housing developments, to improve the character of race relations in these developments, or whatever the case may be). In general, rapport with interviewees is contingent on their understanding of these objectives. This is not invariably so, for some seem to enjoy the occasion for exploring their responses to a situation as interesting in its own right. Nevertheless, it seems to us appropriate that the interviewer provide an informed basis for rapport by clarifying the objectives of the interview.

Although explanation of purpose will naturally differ in detail, it takes much the same form in interviews focused on seemingly most varied situations. The interviewer explains that it is necessary to learn the reactions of people to the particular stimulus situation—a motion picture or radio program, the design of a dwelling or the meeting of an interracial group—in order to help eliminate their defects and enlarge their worth in the future. ("We would like to have your reactions to this film so that future films can be made as interesting as possible. . . ." Or again: "You have probably found that your apartment in this project has both good and bad features. We would like to have you tell us about these so that future housing projects can benefit by your experience.")

From the beginning, the emphasis is put upon the actual experience of the interviewees—their reactions to the situation. They are being asked not to sit as judges, but to report the experiences which can accumulatively help provide a basis for judgment. As we shall presently see, *reports of experience involving evaluations* usually serve the objectives of the interview, whereas *summary evaluations* seldom do.

DEFINING ROLES OF INTERVIEWER AND INTERVIEWEE

The interviewer also explains that he is not himself involved in the situation to be discussed. He is not the producer of the film or radio program, or the architect who has designed the building. He is affectively detached in the sense of not being committed to the situation as it exists, but is concerned only to learn how the interviewees felt about it. He invites critical comments, explaining that there is obviously as great value in learning what proved to be "wrong" with the situation as in learning what was "right" with it. It is his job to learn from their experience, whatever it may have been.

Manifestly, the role which the interviewee comes to define for himself affects his behavior in the interview. It is the task of the interviewer to facilitate the formation of appropriate role definitions and to curb those which are inappropriate. From the beginning, the interviewee is helped to see himself as a witness to his own experience who is being given the opportunity to testify in all pertinent detail rather than to see himself as an experimental guinea pig taking a test, say, of memory. The interviewee is reminded that practically no one can remember every detail of an experience, but that much can be learned from whatever he recalls of his reactions to the situation. Furthermore, since it is he who has had the experience, he alone is in a position to be helpful to others who are yet to have it. As it turns out, once the individual takes active part in the interview, he tends progressively to define his role as that of a forerunner, which often evokes an understandable sense of pride, rather than that of a guinea pig, which arouses resentment. Even a few remarks by the interviewer at the outset can do much to lead to the first rather than the second of these role definitions.

Particularly when he seeks to obtain evaluations of a particular product—say, a film, radio program or architectural design—the interviewer is often inclined to cast interviewees in the role of a critic or judge or technical consultant. He may ask for judgments about the ways in which the product *should* be improved. This type of questioning usually proves to be sterile.[1] Instead of reporting his own experience, the interviewee, in this role, improvises opinions about the probable responses of *others* to the product. He tends to speculate rather than to report. Consider, for example, the following case in point:

> *Int.* If you were producing films like this, what would you show in the film that wasn't shown or what would you leave out?
>
> *A.* I would show the actual facts, but *not to the women,* since they are selfish and would not want their sons and husbands to go.
>
> *B.* *We should* at the same time show pictures of production in this country . . . *to help morale.* The only thing is, it might show the enemy where our plants are.

By asking interviewees to assume the role of scriptwriters, film directors or their equivalent, the interviewer moves them far afield from reports of their actual experience. To be sure, they may welcome the bid to exercise their creative imagination, but often with results which are sufficiently illustrated in the following passage:

> *Int.* What sort of program would you suggest?
>
> *A.* I don't want to class myself as a Nazi, so suppose we take that lamp. Take the lamp and take yourself. That makes you an ally. You get into a heated argument in a room by yourselves, and he says, "I'm a superman— I have 20,000 airplanes, the greatest dive bombers, greatest tanks; I have all sorts of stuff." You come out and say, "I haven't that right now, but I'm going to have it in the very near future." Two people can bring out the different points in conversation—of what we are able to do, bring out what we have already, and then

---

1. See Hovland, Lumsdaine and Sheffield, *Experiments on Mass Communications,* pp. 92-93.

we can bring them to the places of action within a period of a year, or six months or three months. You could use the reaction between two individuals.

Of the various roles which can be assigned to interviewees, that of critic, producer or technical consultant seems to have least to recommend it.

DEFINING THE RELATIONSHIP AMONG INTERVIEWEES

In Chapter VII, dealing with the group interview, we noted the advisability of pointing out that full agreement among interviewees is scarcely to be expected. This calls for only one additional observation. It is useful to make this point clear *from the beginning,* perhaps by a preamble along the following lines.

As everyone knows, people usually have very different opinions about something like this. So if you should hear someone telling of his reaction to the [film] and you have a different slant on it, let's hear about it so that we can have everyone's point of view.

By *anticipating* variability of response as a matter of course, the interviewer helps define a group norm in which conflicts of opinion are not taken as signs of interpersonal conflict. As we have observed, it may prove necessary to reiterate some version of this theme during the interview. But if the expectation of differing opinion or response is stated *only after* a conflict between interviewees is brewing, it will be recognized for what it is: a lame rationalization after the fact by a would-be peacemaker. If, however, it has been presented from the beginning as something that is to be taken for granted, interpersonal tensions that develop later can be more readily resolved by the interviewer, who is then in a position to observe that this is just the kind of difference of opinion which everyone had expected to turn up in the course of the interview.

THE USE OF IDIOM

In everyday life, people generally recognize that age, educational, occupational and class strata have their more or less distinctive vocabularies and styles of speech. It is important that the interviewer not lose sight of these familiar, though often unformulated, patterns of variation.

From the outset, the interviewer can adapt his choice of language to what he knows of the formal education and statuses of interviewees. As the interview proceeds, he will become progressively aware of the idiom current in the group. Although he would be mistaken to emulate this idiom if it is in fact alien to him—the frequent awkwardness of such an attempt often defeats its purpose—he can make use, in his own questions, of distinctive phrases which have turned up in the interview. This is simply to say that when the interviewer speaks in the vernacular, he should retain the colloquialisms which interviewees use to describe their experience.

OPENING QUESTIONS

In connection with each criterion of the focused interview, we have had occasion to consider types of questions designed to get the interview effectively under way. It has been indicated that, in substance, these questions (1) direct attention to the stimulus situation rather than to the response, (2) lead interviewees to specify the aspects of the situation to which they had particularly attended and (3) encourage them to describe their responses to these aspects. The two following examples may be enough to bring back to mind the concrete nature of the opening question and the type of reply which it may elicit.

> *Int.* If you think back on that film that you saw the other day, what part would you say stood out most in your own mind . . . ?
>
> *A.* I think the enthusiasm that the German people showed when Hitler or one of his cohorts spoke at the Reichs-

tag. Why, they were just over-enthusiastic. They remind me of a colored spiritual gathering where they just gave all out and showed we were up against something more than just a plain, ordinary man.

Int. What stood out in your mind as something you will remember about the film?

A. What impressed me was the attack of Poland, women crying, sitting on their knees and praying and crying.

Int. How did you feel when you saw that?

A. Very rotten. I have seen a few films like that. That is the reason I enlisted in the Army and I am right here.

A few words should now be said about a problem of procedure which often arises when an opening question of this kind has been posed. Not infrequently, the interviewee will reply by *listing* various parts of the situation which have caught his eye, without giving any clue to their relative significance for him. In the group interview, there may be an even more extended enumeration of recalled items.

Supplied with what amounts to a preliminary inventory of recall, the interviewer needs to take note of the several items and only later to follow up each of these in turn before moving the interview onto new ground. Particularly in the group interview, the alternative practice of halting the enumeration to develop the comment of one interviewee seems to frustrate the spontaneity of the interview and makes for interruption by others before the first item has in fact been fully explored. A case in point:

Int. What parts do you remember most?

A. I believe that the organization of the German command stood out more in my opinion than anything else and the unorganization or disorder and unpreparedness of the French and Belgian and Dutch people.

Int. What brought out the Nazi organization—do you remember?

A. Well, the way they had things planned out, and just the general organization. That is what impressed me, more or less

> *Int.* How about that?
>
> *B.* I agree, *but I would just like to add a few more things.*
> The first thing that impressed me was their division,
> that is, their propaganda. . . .

It is generally advisable for the interviewer to pause after
his opening question in order to provide occasion for interviewees to indicate their distinctive items of recall and response. He then sorts out the ensuing array of replies and
proceeds to probe each of them. In this way, he maintains a
level of spontaneity in the opening phase of the interview
which can establish the tone for what follows.

Controlling the Expression of Interviewers' Sentiments[2]

Like other professional roles,[3] the role of the interviewer
engaged in social research calls for a blend of detachment
and of interest. As a detached listener, he disciplines himself
to give no overt evidence that his feelings are affected by
what the interviewee says or does; as an interested listener,
he exhibits a capacity for empathy, of being able to enter
understandingly into the experience of the interviewee. This
composite attitude is like the "detached concern" which is a
principal component of the physician's role in relation to his
patients. The interviewer, like the physician, requires sustained discipline to learn this attitude which is in such thor-

---

2. This is one of the few places in which we consider in some detail a
set of problems and practices common to all manner of research interviews
rather than being distinctive of the focused interview. But since this affects
virtually every phase of the interview, it requires more than cursory mention. For discussions of this problem, see Roethlisberger and Dickson, *Management and the Worker*, pp. 285 *ff.;* Maccoby and Maccoby, "The interview: a tool of social science," *op. cit.,* p. 465; Hyman, *Interviewing in Social
Research*, pp. 28-75.

3. For an apposite analysis of "affective neutrality" as an essential component of professional roles, see Talcott Parsons, *Essays in Sociological Theory*
(Glencoe, Illinois: The Free Press, 1951) , esp. Chapter X. Cf. Hyman, *op.
cit.,* 39, who draws a direct comparison between the interviewer and the
physician in this respect.

oughgoing contrast to the patterned expectations governing behavior in most spheres of social life, where the expression of a sentiment by one ordinarily evokes the expression of a sentiment by the other.[4]

From time to time in a protracted interview, the interviewer may find himself tempted to voice his personal opinions or sentiments in response to what is being said. Rather than remain a detached but interested listener, he may want, in effect, to take the role of a teacher by correcting an obviously mistaken allegation of fact, or, observing that certain attitudes are ill-founded, he may feel constrained to set the record straight. Should he yield to feelings of this kind, he will convert the interview from a situation in which interviewees freely describe a set of experiences into a debating society where opinions are pitted against one another or into a classroom where the authoritative teacher informs the students. The interviewer who expresses his own views generally invites spurious reports and defensive remarks or else inhibits certain discussions altogether.

SPURIOUS REPORTS

When an interviewer agrees or disagrees with what an interviewee has said, he is, of course, turning attention to the correctness of responses. He invites proper, rather than authentic, reports. Interviewees become progressively less oriented toward the responses they have actually had and progressively more oriented toward what they have been given to understand is the appropriate response. Consider the following extract from a group interview with soldiers.

A.   [As he turns to a member of the group who has just voiced an opinion.] Pardon me, you didn't see the

---

4. In the course of current research on the sociology of medical education, the Bureau of Applied Social Research has begun to identify the complex processes of didactic and situational learning through which medical students come to incorporate detached concern in their professional selves. It is assumed that equivalent forms of attitudinal learning are required by the sociological interviewer.

whole film. In the beginning did you see the American
General Nimitz, and then Willkie, and they show you
the American soldiers where there is fifteen per cent of
the United States soldiers of German race. Right? That
shows you that the American government is not against
the German people, but it is against the leaders.

Int. It did show that and *I think that point was meant to
be shown.*

Trying to keep the record straight, the interviewer inadvertently allies himself with one perception of the situation: he defines the "correct" perception.

He also exhibits his authoritative position: he *knows* what
was actually in the film as well as the intent of the producers of the film. Note what follows after he has passed
judgment on the validity of a response.

A. It's to stop you from hating the German race.

B. That is the way I took it.

The one soldier reiterates the view which has been sustained by the interviewer and another is quick to say that
he too has had the "right" perception. The interview is on
its way to becoming an occasion for reporting reactions and
opinions which the interviewer will regard as "correct."

DEFENSE OF EGO FEELINGS

The interviewer will sometimes deliver himself of a sentiment or opinion without being aware that he is doing so. He
may think that he is engaged only in helping to draw out to
the full what the speaker is trying to say. But what he regards
as guidance, the interviewee takes as a reflection upon his
intelligence or knowledgeability. The spontaneous flow of
the interview is halted while he tries to maintain his self-
esteem intact by defensively reiterating his original statement.

In the following example, the interviewer supplies what
he considers to be the logical implications of an expressed
point of view and then asks, in effect, whether the speaker
is willing to abide by these implications.

Int. You say we should make a democracy out of Germany.

> In a democracy, the people have the right to choose their own leaders. . . .

Note the didactic formulation of this criterion of a democracy. The attitudinal and affective implications of the interviewee's statement—the kind of material germane to a focused interview—are neglected and the logical implications emphasized. The discussion takes on the character of an exercise in political semantics.

Int. Supposing we were to set up a democracy and then they wanted to choose Hitler as president?

Continuing to draw out the implications of what has been said, the interviewer manages to pass invidious judgment on the soundness of the interviewee's position. Translated, this hypothetical question reads: "Surely you can't mean what you assert; this is a wholly indefensible opinion."

A. *Wait a minute.* What Hitler done, he took children and we should take and mobilize this group and teach them democracy, have a constitution like the United States and make democrats out of them.

The defensive character of the phrase, "wait a minute," signals that a debate is in process. The interviewee maintains his self-esteem by defensive reiteration of his original opinion. And grimly pursued to his last line of retreat by the pertinacious interviewer, he wards off further attack by an explosive monosyllable.

Int. And they wouldn't want to choose a leader like Hitler?
A. No!

In general, it seems preferable to have a further question directed to the affective content of what is being said rather than to pounce upon a logically implicit conclusion.[5] Few devices are better calculated to stem the flow of conversation than that of countering an apparent statement of fact, which is actually the expression of a sentiment, with proof that the alleged fact is simply not true. Should the interviewer adopt this practice, he can await with some confidence a result such as the following.

---

5. Cf. Roethlisberger and Dickson, *op. cit.,* p. 290.

    B. In America a man has the privilege of living in a democracy where, even though he may be of the middle or lower class, he may still reach for and attain positions of high office, whereas in England, the upper class or monied people selfishly hold on to the positions of leadership, never giving the middle or lower class an opportunity to gain such positions. For instance, *a coal miner could never hope to attain a position of high office.*

    Int. What about David Lloyd George: *wasn't he a coal miner?*

    B. Yes, I guess that's true.

What the interviewer hoped to accomplish by his challenge is not at all clear. Perhaps he wanted to learn whether the speaker was able to distinguish between Lloyd George and, say, Aneurin Bevan. Whatever his intentions, the only evident result is the abrupt silencing of an interviewee who, just a moment before, had been highly articulate.

As a rule, the interviewer knows the penalties of criticizing the behavior of interviewees and will not deliberately set about such criticism. Yet he may indict an interviewee when he least intends it. For example, he may unwittingly convey a sense of disappointment over the fact that the interviewee has failed to touch upon certain matters which are pertinent to hypotheses developed in the interview guide. What he intends only as a prod to pertinence is experienced by the interviewee as an indictment. Consider the following case:

    Int. You are all fighting engineers. *How does it happen that not one of you so far has mentioned what the Nazi engineer battalions were doing through all this? Don't you remember any of that?*

The intent of the interviewer is clear enough: he has anticipated that the engineers would be particularly alerted to their counterparts in the German army and wants to learn why this has apparently not occurred. His maladroit observation and question imply, however, that the interviewees have not lived up to his expectations. He intends merely to check an hypothesis and instead manages to censure interviewees for their oversight. They respond to what he has implied and hasten to reassure him that they have indeed had the expected and therefore presumably correct reaction.

A. They go in first and build bridges. That is like I said. They were all in one unison. *I meant to state that.*

The rule that the interviewer should not indicate his own attitudes toward the subject matter under discussion or toward the interviewee is now so well established that it is described as a cardinal principle of the interviewing art.[6] It is a rule which interviewers are taught from the outset of their training and, therefore, they will not *knowingly* violate it. Since violations nevertheless do occur, through inadvertence rather than unrestrained intent, it may be useful to recapitulate some of the interviewing practices in the course of which the interviewer unwittingly communicates his sentiments or opinions.

1. The interviewer thinks that he is only supplying needed information to the interviewee whereas he is, in social fact, implicitly lending his support to one rather than another response as appropriate or valid.
2. He thinks that he is only helping the interviewee to trace out the full implications of the report when he is actually impugning the interviewee's knowledge or intelligence.
3. He thinks that he is only helping to straighten out the details of the interviewee's report, but is instead accusing him of failing to recognize inconsistencies.
4. He thinks that he is only helping the interviewee to provide data bearing upon hypotheses in the study when he is actually indicting him for being remiss as a reporter of experience.

The Treatment of Interviewees' Questions

On occasion, the interviewee will attempt to reverse roles by directing questions to the *interviewer.* When these have

---

6. Maccoby and Maccoby, *op. cit.,* p. 465.

to do with the interview or the research—their purposes, auspices or probable duration, for example—they present no particular problem of interviewing procedure. Direct answers serve to orient the interviewee without prejudicing his reports of experience. But often, the questions are of quite a different kind, being designed to seek out the interviewer's feelings, attitudes or perceptions. ("How do you feel about . . . ?" or "Do you think that . . . ?") If the interviewer were to respond to the manifest content of these questions and express his own sentiments, he would only create the problems reviewed in the preceding section.

The attempted reversal of roles is particularly apt to occur at those points in the interview when continued self-exploration by the interviewee would be most revealing. The questions often reflect his emotional blockage. He may be reluctant to explore his own feelings because they are painful or embarrassing or because they are so diffuse that he cannot easily put them into words. By directing attention to the interviewer, he diverts attention from himself. He hopes, at times, that the answer will provide the "correct" formulation of his own vague feelings. Psychological groping finds rhetorical expression in the form of a question.

When this type of situation arises, it is incumbent upon the interviewer to avoid responding to the ostensible content of the question and yet to encourage the interviewee to continue with his report. In general, he will find it possible to achieve this double objective by *restating the implied meaning of the question and redirecting the revised question to the interviewee.* The restatement recognizes the legitimacy of the question, even though it is not being answered. The restatement also communicates the tacit conviction that the interviewee himself can answer his own question and that the interviewer is interested in his doing so. This sort of stimulation is often all that is needed for the report to continue, as can be seen in the following instance of this technique of countering a question with a question:

> *A.* Did the Germans think that the girl was working with them?
>
> *Int. You mean it wasn't clear* whether she was working with the Germans or not?
>
> *A.* That's right. You remember when. . . .

Rather than answer *A*'s question, which would reduce the likelihood of ferreting out the way in which he structured this sequence in a film, the interviewer responds to the *implied* meaning of the question: "You mean it wasn't clear . . . ?" This provides an opportunity for the interviewee to characterize the aspects of this sequence which led to his confusion.

The same procedure can be effectively adapted to the requirements of the group interview by restating the implied meanings in the form of extensive questions directed to the group at large. This has the further advantage of extending the basis for discussion while still affording the original speaker an occasion to report his feelings.

> *A.* I didn't like the voices. Were they the real men or imitations?
>
> *Int. How many* thought it was the actual men speaking?
>
> *B.* I did.
>
> *A.* I object to the idea of having them impersonated. A continuous flow of talk is better and more effective than cutting in with a phony character.

By presenting the issue implied in the question, the interviewer elicits an expression of attitude by the interviewee, without structuring the situation for him. As is often the case, the question here turns out to be merely a prelude to the voicing of an attitude which finds ready expression when the interviewer does not answer the question but only restates its implied content.

We observed earlier that questions about the interview or research, as distinct from questions about the interviewer's sentiments or perceptions, ought to be answered directly. It should be noted now that questions of the second kind, which require restatement rather than answer, are sometimes couched in a form that resembles questions of the first kind. If the interviewer is not alerted to this practice, as in the following passage, he will be inclined to answer the seeming request for information and thus shape the perceptions or responses of the interviewee.

A. I would like to ask you a question.

Int. That is fair enough.

A. *Do you really think the show was meant* for the engineers or for the Army as a whole?

At this point, the interviewer could reply with a restatement of the substantial content of the question: "Did you get any impression that it was meant specifically for engineers or for the Army in general?" Instead, he assumes that this is merely a request for information ancillary to the interview and proceeds as follows:

Int. I am sorry if I didn't make that clear. I should have. This movie is shown to all the men in the Army, you see; the whole series of seven films is shown to all the men in the Army.

A. The infantry?

Int. Yes, *not just for the engineers.*

A. *That is the way I thought of the picture*—as a whole. I didn't pick out certain groups.

By answering the question, the interviewer tends to establish the "appropriate" perception of the film. He has failed to recognize that the question is a disguised request for guidance to "correct" responses. Guided by this "standard," the interviewee is likely to refrain from reporting the perceptions he may in fact have had of matters in the film which relate to his own role as an engineer.

In short, it is the business of the interviewer to listen to the hints contained in questions addressed to him and so to restate these as to have them further elucidated.

⟩ Selected
⟩ Bibliography

Books

Advertising Research Foundation. *Focus Groups: Issues and Approaches*. New York: ARF, 1985.

Bellenger, Danny N., Kenneth L. Bernhardt, and J. L. Goldstrucker. *Qualitative Research in Marketing*. Chicago: American Marketing Association, 1976.

Dexter, Lewis A. *Elite and Specialized Interviewing*. Evanston, IL: Northwestern University Press, 1970.

Focus Research Group [entire Issue] *Studies in Family Planning* 1981, Vol. 12.

Goldman, Alfred E., and Susan Schwartz McDonald. *The Group Depth Interview: Principles and Practice*. Englewood Cliffs, NJ: Prentice-Hall, 1987.

Gordon, Raymond L. *Interviewing: Strategy, Techniques, and Tactics*. Homewood, IL: The Dorsey Press, 1969.

Greenbaum, Thomas L. *The Practical Handbook and Guide to Focus Group Research*. Lexington, MA: D. C. Heath, 1988.

Higginbotham, James B., and Keith K. Cox, eds. *Focus Group Interviews: A Reader*. Chicago: American Marketing Association, 1979.

Krueger, Richard A., Ardis C. Hutchins, and Gail D. Olney. *Focus Group Interviewing for Architects and Interior Designers*. Saint Paul: Research in Design, 1985.

Krueger, Richard A. *Focus Groups: A Practical Guide for Applied Research.* Newbury Park, CA.: Sage Publications, 1988.

Merton, Robert K., Marjorie Fiske, and Patricia L. Kendall. *The Focused Interview.* New York: Free Press, 1956, 1990.

Mishler, Eliot G. *Research Interviewing: Context and Narrative.* Cambridge, MA: Harvard University Press, 1986.

Morgan, David L. *Focus Groups as Qualitative Research.* Newbury Park, CA: Sage Publications, 1988.

Rovner, Mark J., and William A. Galston. *One Year to Go: Citizens' Attitudes in Iowa and New Hampshire.* Washington DC: Roosevelt Center for American Policy Studies, 1987.

Stewart, Charles, and William B. Cash, Jr. *Interviewing: Principles and Practices.* 4th ed. Dubuque: William C. Brown, 1985.

Templeton, Jane F. *Focus Groups: A Guide for Marketing and Advertising Professionals.* Chicago: Probus Pub. Co., 1987.

Whyte, William Foote. *Learning from the Field: A Guide from Experience.* Beverly Hills, CA: Sage Publications, 1984.

Zuckerman, Harriet A. *Scientific Elite: Nobel Laureates in the United States.* New York: Free Press, 1977.

Articles

Baker, Philip N. "Focus group interviewing: The real constituency." *Journal of Data Collection* (1985), 25:14–23.

Basch, Philip N. "Focus group interview: An underutilized research technique for improving theory and practice in health education." *Health Education Quarterly* (1987), 14:411–448.

Beck, Leif C., W. L. Trombetta, and S. Share. "Using focus group sessions before decisions are made." *North Carolina Medical Journal* (1986), 47:73–74.

Beckett, Kathleen. "Focus groups: A market research tool." *Credit Union Executive* (1985), 25:8–12.

Bers, Trudy H. "Exploring institutional images through focus group interviews." *New Directions for Institutional Research,* No. 54 (1987), 14:19–29.

Bers, Trudy H., and Kerry Smith. "Focus groups and community college research: Lessons from a study of nontraditional students." *Community College Review* (1988), 15:52–58.

Bortree, William H. "Focus groups reduce innovation risks." *Bank Marketing* (1986), 18:18–24.

Byrne, Andrew J. "Focus groups: Valuable data, but not basis of sales forecasts." *Direct Marketing* (1984), 46:66–72.

Calder, Bobby J. "Focus groups and the nature of qualitative market research." *Journal of Marketing Research* (1977), 14:353–364.

Cohen, Barry. "Designing a sound system for a focus group facility." *Applied Marketing Research* (1988), 28:39–43.

Cora, Ellen C. "Use respondent facades to increase focus group productivity." *Medical Marketing and Media* (1986), 21:11–18.

Cox, Keith K., James B. Higginbotham, and J. Burton. "Applications of focus group interviews in marketing." *Journal of Marketing* (1976), 40:77–80.

Davis, Christine S. "Agricultural focus groups: A unique approach." *Applied Marketing Research* (1988), 28:53–58.

Diamond, W. D., and J. P. Gagnon. "Obtaining pharmacy class feedback through the use of focus group interviews." *American Journal of Pharmaceutical Education* (1985), 49:49–54.

Droste, T. "Focus groups provide insight into marketplace." *Hospitals* (1988), 62:45–46.

Fern, Edward F. "The use of focus groups for idea generation: The effects of group size, acquaintanceship, and moderator on response-quantity and quality." *Journal of Marketing Research* (1982), 19:1–13.

————. "Why do focus groups work 2: A review and integration of small group process theories." *Advances in Consumer Research* (1982), 9:444–452.

————. "Focus groups: A review of some contradictory evidence, implications, and suggestions for future research." *Advances in Consumer Research* (1983), 10:121–126.

Festervand, Troy A. "An introduction and application of focus group research to the health care industry." *Health Marketing Quarterly* (1985), 2:199–209.

Flesch, Regina. "A guide to interviewing of the bereaved: The focused interview schedule." *Journal of Thanatology* (1975), 3:143–159.

Folch-Lyon, E., L. de la Macorra, and S. B. Schearer. "Focus group and survey research on family planning in Mexico." *Studies in Family Planning* (1981), 12:409–432.

Folch-Lyon, E., and J. F. Trost. "Conducting focus group sessions." *Studies in Family Planning* (1981), 12:443–449.

Gage, Theodore J. "Theories differ on use of focus group." *Advertising Age* (1980), 5:5–19, 20–22.

Gelb, Betsy D., and Richard J. Cheney. "Pre-testing jurors' reactions to corporate marketing decisions." *Journal of Public Policy & Marketing* (1986), 5:97–104.

Goodman, R. Irwin. "Focus group interviews in media product testing." *Educational Technology* (1984), 24:39–44.

Hansler, Daniel F., and Catherine Cooper. "Focus groups: New dimension in feasibility study." *Fund Raising Management* (1986), 17:78–82.

Harlow, Glenda W. "A study of the usefulness of the focused interview as a method to determine if secondary principals exhibit rational behavior in the decision-making process." *Dissertation Abstracts International* (1980), 40:5267.

Harris, Robert J. "Focus groups offer six 'guidelines' for Black-oriented ads." *Marketing News* (October 16, 1981), pp. 5, 14.

Heath, Robert L. "Are focus groups a viable tool for PR practitioners to help their companies establish corporate responsibility?" *Public Relations Quarterly* (Winter 1987/88), 32:24–28.

Heimann-Ratain, Giselle, Molly Hanson, and Stephen M. Peregay. "The role of focus group interviews in designing a smoking prevention program." *Journal of School Health* (1985), 55:13–16.

Herman, Raymond O, "Focus groups: Bank management beware." *Bank Marketing* (1982), 14:20–32.

Hisrich, R. D., and P. M. Peters. "Focus groups: An innovative marketing-research technique." *Hospital and Health Services Administration* (1982), 27:8–21.

Hutt, Roger W. "The focus group interview: A technique for counseling small business clients." *Journal of Small Business Management* (1979), 17:15–19.

Inglis, Robert C. "In-depth data: Using focus groups to study industrial markets." *Business Marketing* (1987), 72:78–82.

Karns, David, Harper A. Roehm, Joseph F. Castellano, and George B. Moore. "Using focus groups to monitor clients' views." *Journal of Accountancy* (1988), 166:148–152.

Keller, Keryl L., et al. "Assessing beliefs about and needs of senior citizens using the focus group interview: A qualitative approach." *Health Education* (1987), 18:44–49.

Keown, Charles. "Focus groups research: Tool for the retailer." *Journal of Small Business Management* (1983), 21:59–65.

Langer, Judith, and Susan Miller. "The ideal focus group facility." *Journal of Data Collection* (1985), 25:34–37.

Lindgren, John H., Jr., and William J. Kehoe. "Focus groups: Approaches, procedures, and implications." *Journal of Retail Banking* (1981), 3:16–22.

Lorence, James, and Bryan Hendricks. "Is innovative teaching more effective? Testing the focus group strategy in the freshman American survey." *History Teacher* (1979), 12:187–211.

Lorz, Michael F. "Focus group research in a winning campaign." *Public Relations Review* (1984), 10:28–38.

Lubet, Margery J. "Focus group research: Planning is the key." *Bank Marketing* (1982), 14:17–20.

Lydecker, Toni H. "Focus group dynamics." *Association Management* (1986), 38:73–78.

Markey, Karen. "Online catalogue use: Results of surveys and focus group interviews in several libraries." *OCLC Online Computer Library Center* (March 31, 1983), 3 vols.

McDaniel, Carl. "Focus groups—Their role in the marketing research process." *Akron Business & Economic Review* (1979), 10:14–19.

McDermott, Dennis R. "Assessing future directions for designing an academic program through focus group interviews." *Journal of Professional Services Marketing* (1987), 2:113–118.

McQuarrie, Edward F., and Shelby H. McIntyre. "Focus groups and the development of new products by technologically driven companies." *Journal of Product Innovation* (1986), 3:40–47.

————. "What focus groups can and cannot do: A reply to Seymour." *Journal of Product Innovation Management* (1987), 4:55–60.

Merton, Robert K. "The focussed interview and focus groups: Continuities and discontinuities." *Public Opinion Quarterly* (1987), 51:550–566.

Merton, Robert K., and Patricia L. Kendall, "The focused interview." *American Journal of Sociology* (1946), 51:541–557.

Modic, Stanley J., and Perry Pascarella. "Focus group . . . Motivation vs. machines." *Industry Week* (July 4, 1977), 194:50–54.

Morgan, David L., and Margaret T. Spanish. "Focus groups: A new tool for qualitative research." *Qualitative Sociology* (1984), 7:253–270.

Morris, Jon D., and Albert B. Smith III. "Using focus groups to evaluate instructional media: A case study." *Educational Technology* (1988), 28:27–32.

Munn, Henry L., and William L. Opdyke. "Group interviews reveal consumer buying behavior." *Journal of Retailing* (Fall 1961), pp. 26–31.

Murray, Simon. "Focus groups by phone: A better way to research health care." *Marketing News* (August 29, 1988), 22:47–48.

Nasser, David. "How to run a focus group." *Public Relations Journal* (1988), 44:33–34.

Nelson, J. E., and N. T. Frontczak. "How acquaintanceship and analyst can influence focus group results." *Journal of Advertising* (1988), 17:41–48.

Pramualratana, Anthony, Napaporn Havanon, and John Knodel. "Exploring the normative basis for marriage in Thailand: An example from focus group research." *Journal of Marriage and the Family* (1985), 47:203–210.

Quiriconi, Roy J., and Richard E. Dorgan. "Respondent personalities: Insight for better focus groups." *Journal of Data Collection* (1985), 25:20–23.

Reynolds, Fred D., and Deborah K. Johnson. "Validity of focus-group findings." *Journal of Advertising Research* (1978), 18: 21–24.

Rigler, Edith. "Focus on focus groups." *ABA Journal of Banking* (1987), 97:96–100.

Schearer, S. B. "The value of focus group research for social-action programs." *Studies in Family Planning* (1981), 12:407–408.

Seymour, Daniel T. "Focus groups and the development of new products by technologically driven companies: A comment." *Journal of Product Innovation Management* (1987), 4:40–54.

Simon, Murray. "Physician focus groups require special techniques." *Marketing News* (January 30, 1987), pp. 21–22.

Stycos, J. M. "A critique of focus group and survey research: The machismo case." *Studies in Family Planning* (1981), 12:450–456.

Suyono, H., N. Piet, F. Stirling, and J. Ross. "Family planning attitudes in Indonesia: Findings from focus group research." *Studies in Family Planning* (1981), 12:409–432.

Tynan, Caroline A., and Jennifer L. Drayton. "Conducting focus groups—A guide for first time users." *Marketing Intelligence and Planning* (1988), 6:5–9.

Welch, Joe L. "Focus groups for restaurant research." *Cornell Hotel and Restaurant Association Quarterly* (1985), 26: 78–85.

—————. "Researching marketing problems and opportunities with focus groups." *Industrial Marketing Management* (1985), 14:245–253.

Wheatley, Kimbal L., and William A. Flexner. "Dimensions that make focus groups work." *Marketing News* (May 9, 1988), 22: 16–17.

White, Pat. "The student-focused interview." *Journal of the National Association of College Admissions Counselors* (1979), 23:22–24.

Winton, Pamela J., and Donald B. Bailey, Jr. "The family-focused interview: A collaborative mechanism for family assessment and goal-setting." *Journal of the Division for Early Childhood* (1988), 12:195–207.

Zimmerman, Juliet G., and Robert N. Zelnio. "Listening is the key to more productive focus group sessions." *Medical Marketing & Media* (1985), 20:84–88.

Zuckerman, Harriet A. "Interviewing an ultra-elite." *Public Opinion Quarterly* (1972), 36:159–175.

Index